MADONNA

THE ILLUSTRATED BIOGRAPHY BY DEBBI VOLLER

I dedicate this book to both my mother and my husba
two of the coolest people in the universe.
Debbi Voller, August 1988

1 2 3 4 5 6 7 8 9 10 11

ISBN 0.7119.2185.7 Order No: OP45905

Exclusive distributors:

Book Sales Limited
8/9 Frith Street, London W1V 5TZ, UK.

Music Sales Corporation
225 Park Avenue South, New York, N.Y. 10003, USA.

Music Sales Pty Limited
120 Rothschild Avenue, Rosebery, NSW 2018, Australia.

To the Music Trade only:
Music Sales Limited
8/9 Frith Street, London W1V 5TZ, UK.

Picture credits:
L Busacca: P53 (BR).
LFI: Front Cover; P2, P8, P17, P20 (R), P21, P23 (T&B), P24, P29, P30 (L&R), P33, P34 (R), P37, (L), P38 (TR), P39 (L&R), P41, P42, P44 (R), P47, P50, P51, P52 (L), P55 (inset), P56, P60, P63, (T&B), P64, P70 (B), P70 (B), P71 (T), P75 (T), P78 (TC), P80 (TL&R), P88, (B), P90, (L&R), P93 (T&B), P97 (T), P98 (TL), P98 (B), P100 (TL, TR, B), P101 (T&B).
Photo G: P6, P7, P11, P16, P22, P25, P27, P36, P40 (T), P48, P52 (R), P57, P71 (B×4), P74, P77 (B), P78 (C), P78 (BL), P83, P85 (T), P87 (T & inset).
Pictorial Press: P4, P9, P10, P13, P14, P18, P19 (L&R), P20 (L), P31, P35, P37 (TR&B), P38 (L), P40 (BL), P43, P44 (BL), P45, P46, P53 (TL&R), P54, P55, P58, P59, P65, P66, P67 (TR), P70 (T). P72, P73, P75 (B), P76, P77 (T×2), P80, (BL&R), P81 (L&R), P82 (L&R), P84, P85 (B), P89, P91, P92, P95, P96, P97 (BL, B), P98 (T), P99.
Gabor Scott: P12, P28 (L&R), P38 (BR), P61.
Starfile: P96.

Printed in the United Kingdom by Ebenezer Baylis and Son Ltd, Worcester.

"I want to rule the world. Every time I reach a new peak, I see a new one I want to climb. It's like I can't stop. Maybe I should rest and admire the view, but I can't. I've got to keep on pushing. Why? I don't know. I don't know what motivates me. I just know I've got to do it."

Madonna attempts to describe the one quality which the whole world would agree she has. Ambition. She's not ruthlessly ambitious, not a cold and calculating opportunist, not a manipulative, exploiting egomaniac – more of a dedicated dreamer who, from an early age, was determined to give her Hollywood heroes and heroines a run for their money. Madonna radiates an aura of ambition and wears it with all the glamour and flirtatious sexuality of Marilyn Monroe, "I want

to be a symbol of something. That's what I think when I think of conquering. It's that you stand for something. I mean, as far as I'm concerned, Marilyn Monroe conquered the world. She stands for something."

And what would Madonna like to stand for? " . . . dreams and magic and things that are happy," are the "positive life-messages" that she wants to put across. "I have a real innocence inside and a love for life and a good sense of humour. I think a lot of people are

afraid to express themselves that way, so they feel they can attach themselves to an innocence and joy." Naïve but noble Hollywood ideals.

Madonna developed that aura of hers with all the energy and focus of a bullet train, speeding towards the great beyond. "I was a little girl from Michigan and I had a dream and I worked really hard and my dream came true." Or, to put it another way, "I basically came from nowhere and scratched and clawed my way to the top."

Madonna's shining aura inspires a mixed bag of emotions and judgements. In the right hand corner, there are the millions of worldwide 'wannabes' who hail her as their rôle model, and in the left hand corner, the Madonna-bashing hacks with their crude boxing gloves, intent on putting her down and building her into a bimbo, an airhead monster, a veritable bride of Frankenstein.

"I realised I had created a monster who would turn on me," declared Camille Barbone dramatically, Madonna's ex-manager from way back, and interestingly enough, just about the only person ever to turn on her with a spiteful dish-the-dirt exclusive for the gutter press. Betrayed by one of her own sex — but never by the men in her life she is supposed to have used and abused. None of them really has a bad word to say about her in retrospect.

For an honest appraisal of the true spirit behind Myth America, you have to look to the friends and associates who have worked closely with her.

"She's a nice person. She's smart. She's dedicated. She's as talented as hell. She's prolific. She's compassionate. She's not this person everybody thinks she is," gushes Pat Leonard, musical director of the Who's That Girl Tour and one of her co-writers.

"She's warm, thoughtful, dedicated, full of humour, vegetarian, intelligent, great looking and has a voice that reflects all of the above. And one day she'll be President," bids fond friend Chrissie Hynde of The Pretenders. Who would you rather believe?

Madonna is, quite simply, a woman who is not afraid to compete in the male-dominated music world as a woman. She combined a saucy, belly button femininity with a smart, competitive mentality and came up trumps. And while America's Moral Majority had heart attacks and tried to get her records banned; while the press had a field day slinging mud at the wanton hot stuff that landed in their greedy laps, America's now reputable *Rolling Stone* magazine merely sat back with a smile on its face and declared her "a lovably subversive pop presence."

But the bottom line of course is that in these so-called enlightened times of sexual equality, ambition is still an undesirable quality in a woman. Hell hath no fury like a threatened male ego.

"Is Madonna ruthless?" ponders Seymour Stein, President of Sire Records and the man who first signed Madonna. "I don't know about ruthless. She's a woman. When men are ambitious, they're ambitious. When women are ambitious, they're ruthless. There's no ego problem there; she's in a hurry, but she's very, very serious about what she does. She knows what she wants. Her talent has really been obscured because of the fuss about everything else."

Madonna agrees that "people are intimidated by women who are incredibly ambitious . . . it's easier to deal with girls who aren't," and has described Warner Brothers as being "a hierarchy of old men," and "a chauvinistic environment to be working in." At first she had to wage a constant battle to prove that she had more to offer than a one-off girl singer. "That is something that happens when you're a girl. It wouldn't have happened to Prince or Michael Jackson."

Male rock sex symbols, from Presley to Prince, have never really had to put up with their onstage sexual antics stealing all the attention from their musical prowess. "People have this idea that if you're sexual and beautiful and provocative, then there's nothing else you could possibly offer. People have always had that image about women," says Madonna. "And while it might have seemed like I was behaving in a stereotypical way, at the same time, I was also masterminding it. I was in control of everything I was doing, and I think that when people realised that, it confused them.

"It's not like I was saying 'Don't pay attention to the clothes – to the lingerie – I'm wearing.' Actually, the fact that I was wearing those clothes was meant to drive home the point that you can be sexy and strong at the same time."

Madonna's offbeat, upfront sense of humour has backfired on her badly on several momentous occasions. Like the time back in early 1985 when a journalist asked her if, as a Catholic, she found it difficult deciding to lose her virginity. A very personal question, to which she cheekily replied, "Oh no. I thought of it as a career move." Everyone took that as gospel.

"People either think I have no sense of humour or they misunderstand it. I can remember in interviews I did early in my career, I'd say the most outrageous things and people thought I was serious." People still misunderstand Madonna, but that's fine by her. "I don't expect everyone to get everything that I'm about. It's part of the mystery and that way people keep discovering things about me."

The little girl that started this whole mega-successful ball rolling, still sits comfortably inside the woman that has become the star. Many people have said of Madonna that beneath that aura of confidence and control lies a fragile and vulnerable child-woman.

"I never met anyone who has such a focus. She goes right for it and she gets what she wants. But I think behind all that is a little tiny girl inside," observed Rosanna Arquette, who starred with Madonna in the film *Desperately Seeking Susan*.

The dreams and the magic and the innocence are as much a part of Madonna's make-up as her pop siren, screen goddess and businesswoman persona. At the end of the day, she has Little Nonni (the nickname her father gave her as a child) to thank for her success – perhaps more than anyone else.

"When I was a child I always thought that the world was mine, that it was a stomping ground for me, full of opportunities. I always had the attitude that I was going to go out into the world and do all the things I wanted to do, whatever that was ... that I was going to get out there and take a bite of the big forest."

Little Nonni's childhood was the proverbial yellow brick road; long and winding and riddled with pitfalls, overshadowed by the dark and guilt ridden hang-ups that go hand in hand with a Catholic upbringing. The big forest was full of demons, some of which still haunt Madonna to this very day.

Madonna Louise Veronica Ciccone was born on August 16 1959, in Bay City, Detroit, "a little smelly town in northern Michigan full of chemical dumps." Her family later moved to Pontiac, and then to a city north of Detroit. "Those are all car factory cities, so everybody's families worked in the car factories."

She was the third and eldest daughter of a lower-middle class Italian/American family of six, born to a Chrysler

engineer, Sylvio, and his wife, Madonna. "My father is a first-generation Italian from the Southern part of Italy. My grandparents weren't very educated and I think in a way they represented an old life-style that he didn't want to have anything to do with.

"He came from a very poor family and lived in a Pittsburgh ghetto. He was the youngest of six boys and the only one who got a college education ... he got an engineering degree and wanted us to have a better life than he did."

One of Little Nonni's earliest memories was of her parents twisting together to records by Chubby Checker and Sam Cooke but, growing up in Detroit, there was really only one kind of music for Nonni to get into – the soul sound of the locally based Motown label.

"We lived in a real integrated neighbourhood. We were one of the only white families, and all the kids had Motown and black stuff. And they had yard dances in their backyards, little 45 turntables and a stack of records, and everyone just danced in the driveway and the back yard ... I really liked The Shirelles, The Ronettes, Martha Reeves And The Vandellas, and The Supremes they're the quintessential pop songs."

1959/1971

Young Madonna puts on a brave face despite all her feelings of insecurity.

Nonni was a five-year-old Motown fan, but when it came to dancing, it was the diminutive Shirley Temple who captured her imagination. Nonni tried to follow in her footsteps and teach her friends to do the same. She was happy when she was dancing in the street. At home, things were a different story . . .

Her father's strict, disciplinarian ideals, however well intentioned, allowed little breathing space for a child to be a child, and Little Nonni found herself going through a rebellious, morbid phase of "wanting really badly either to . . . find out my parents weren't my real parents – so I could be an orphan and feel sorry for myself – or I wanted everyone to die in a car accident so I wouldn't have parents to tell me what do. My dad used to send me to my room and I'd slam the door and say 'I hate you . . .'"

But Little Nonni adored her mother, and her idea of Heaven was creeping into her parents' bedroom when she couldn't sleep at night, and crawling between the sheets with them, despite the usual protests from her father. "I felt really lonely and forlorn, even though my brothers and sisters were in my room with me . . . my mother had a really beautiful red, silky nightgown and I remember rubbing against it and going to sleep."

Little Nonni's idea of Hell was the devil, whom she believed lived in their basement, and tried to grab hold of her ankles as she ran up the stairs. Meanwhile, God was "watching everything I did."

In 1966 when she was six-and-a-half, Nonni really did have every reason to feel sorry for herself. Her mother died of breast cancer after nearly a year in hospital, tragically misdiagnosed by doctors.

"My mother tried to keep her fear deep inside her and not let us know," remembers Madonna. "Once she was sitting on the couch and I climbed on her back and said, 'Play with me' and she wouldn't. She couldn't. I got really angry with her and started pounding her with my fist and saying, 'Why are you doing this?' Then I realised she was crying . . ."

Perhaps it's easy to see where Madonna gets her bizarre sense of humour from when you learn that just before she died, her mother "asked for a hamburger because she couldn't eat anything for so long, and I thought that was very funny."

Madonna has described her mother as being a sweet, beautiful, forgiving and angelic woman, whom she loved a lot. "Madonna is my mother's name . . . it's very rare for an Italian Catholic mother to name her daughter after her – especially as it's a rare

name, so I think in a way that maybe it was meant to happen that she died when I was so young."

The name Madonna holds a wealth of meaning: "It means virgin, mother, mother of earth, someone who is very pure and innocent but someone who's very strong." Madonna believes that, in some mysterious way, her mother's spirit lives on inside her. But she has also said that " . . . my big demons will always be there. One of the hardest things I've faced in life was the death of my mother and that's something I really haven't gotten over to this day. I carry many deep wounds inside . . ."

Sylvio Ciccone could not possibly cope with looking after six children and holding down his job with Chrysler, so emergency measures were taken and Little Nonni and her brothers and sisters were packed off to relatives for a couple of months, until a housekeeper was hired and they were all allowed to return home.

But now the big forest felt like an awfully lonely place to be, and Nonni experienced "an intense longing to fill a sort of emptiness."

To try and mend the heartbreak and insulate herself against further grief, she resolved that "if I couldn't have a mother to take care of me, then I was gonna take care of myself." She also determined that, far from feeling left out in the cold, she was going to make sure she had "a special life." Nonni had set the wheels of the Madonna dream machine in motion.

"I knew I had to be extra specially super-charged to get what I wanted because we had to share everything. I did all I could to really stand out and that nurtured a lot of confidence and ambition."

Madonna started to enjoy the luxury of being "the main female of the house" because, despite the fact that her brothers and sisters were also constantly vying for attention, she knew that "being charming in a feminine sort of way could get me a lot of things, and I milked it for everything I could." The tragedy of her mother's death brought Madonna closer to her father and she became daddy's little girl. "There was no woman between us."

But her tomboy sister and older brothers didn't like the way she managed to wrap her father round her little finger with her feminine wiles, and started ganging up on her.

They picked on her, called her a sissy and punished her for her precociousness by hanging her up on the clothes line by her underpants.

The fab 'n' groovy fashion-conscious sixties were beginning to make a deep impression on Madonna, even if she was too young to join in the fun. When Nancy Sinatra's classic song 'These Boots Are Made For Walkin'' was released, Madonna was entranced by her image; "the go-go boots, mini-skirt, blonde hair and fake eyelashes . . . when I was younger I really liked girl singers like Lulu and those kind of innocent, angelic voices."

The first two records she ever bought were 'Incense And Peppermints' by Strawberry Alarm Clock, and 'The Letter' by The Box Tops in 1967. Her snooty brothers now found a new way to torment her. "They told me pop music was a pile of shit, they scratched my records so that I couldn't play them. It only made me love pop more."

Meanwhile, a whole string of housekeepers came and went in the Ciccone household, none of whom Madonna liked – except one – and she looked very much like their departed mother, "sorta like Natalie Wood . . . we all thought our father was going to marry her."

One evening, when Madonna was nine, Sylvio announced that he was going to get married. But not to the housekeeper they had all been rooting for.

If Madonna's real mother had been the good fairy in her life, the new housekeeper-turned-stepmother slipped neatly into the role of the Wicked Witch of the East. "She was really gung-ho, very strict . . . it was hard to accept her as an authority figure and the new number one female in my father's life. He wanted us to call her Mom, not her first name." Madonna choked at the effort.

Now there were two disciplinarians in the family and two new arrivals – the six children soon became eight. Madonna had clearly lost her battle for supremacy. Instead she found a growing desire to escape her Michigan hometown and find that "special life" elsewhere.

"We all had to go to church every morning before we went to school. When we got home, we'd get changed, do our chores, do our homework and eat supper. I wasn't even allowed to watch television until I was into my teens. My father didn't like us having idle time on our hands. If we didn't have homework he'd

find us something to do around the house. He was very adamant about being productive."

Sylvio Ciccone also insisted that each of his children learn to play a musical instrument. Madonna had little interest in plonking away at piano keys for hours on end and, rather than turn up to lessons, would run away and "hide in a ditch."

When she was nine, Madonna "discovered boys" and received her first Valentine card, rather disappointedly, from someone she didn't much fancy. Her eyes were busy popping out at an older boy in the Fifth Grade called Ronny Howard who "had white-blond hair and sky blue eyes. I wrote his name all over my sneakers and on the playground. I used to take off the top part of my uniform and chase him around."

Madonna was starting to express her sensuality, a side of herself which she claims to have been in touch with since the age of five. It was an inevitable and natural discovery. Unless of course you are Catholic. Madonna's grandmother used to beg her to love Jesus and be a good girl, "I grew up with two images of woman, the Virgin and the whore. Father told me to stay away from boys, which made me even more interested."

Madonna created two more images of woman: the Brownie and the Campfire girl. As a young Brownie, Madonna knew how to conduct herself, but once she graduated to Campfire girl she used to "camp out with all the boys and get into trouble."

When she was 10, Madonna started giving raunchy dance lessons to boys. "I remember the first guy I gave lessons to. The song was 'Honky Tonk Women' by The Rolling Stones and it was really sexy, really stomping and grinding." Her current heroine was Motown goddess, Diana Ross.

Madonna as a High School cheerleader – but dance always came first.

Madonna was no late developer, but claims she was misunderstood. "When I was growing up I remember liking my body and not being ashamed of it. I remember liking boys and not feeling inhibited. I never played little games, if I liked a boy I'd confront him. Maybe it comes from having older brothers and sharing the bathroom. But when you're that aggressive in junior high, the boys get the wrong impression. They mistake your forwardness for sexual promiscuity."

Not surprisingly perhaps, Madonna started to fantasise about Catholic symbolism. She had her first adolescent crush on Jesus Christ himself, "He was like a movie star, my favourite idol of all." She chose Veronica as her confirmation name after the woman who wiped the face of Jesus ... "which I thought was really dramatic." And she wanted to become a nun. "I thought nuns were very beautiful ... I saw them as really pure, disciplined, above average people. They had these really serene faces. Nuns are sexy."

Though she was fast growing into a flirtatious young lady, Madonna's self-image at this time wasn't glamorous at all. Far from seeing herself as a budding Monroe, she cast herself in the role of a bedraggled Cinderella, a victim of domestic circumstance and hand-me-down rags.

"There was a lot of responsibility on me. I'd come home from school and there'd be nappies on the line and mouths to feed," and all the time she kept saying to herself, "I have this stepmother and I have this work and I never go out and I don't have any pretty dresses."

It was a time of anger. From her junior high school days, right up until the last year of high school, Madonna's wrath fuelled her desire to fight back and make an impression on the world. She felt lost and rejected. She couldn't find the love she needed at home, and she was searching for someone to identify with as her childhood slipped away. "My parents weren't worldly and I didn't know many people who were ... I couldn't identify with anyone, so I wandered aimlessly."

She took some of her frustration out on her class mates when she was appointed hall monitor, by abusing her position and reporting others for misconduct – when they hadn't actually done anything. "The nuns forgave me for a lot of the things I did because they thought, 'Well, she doesn't have a mother and her father's never there' and I knew it so I milked it."

Madonna went to three different Catholic schools, all very strict and regimented, but good breeding grounds for ambition. They instilled in her "an incentive to win – to aim for the top rung of the ladder," and blessed her with "an inner strength."

Madonna wasn't too sure exactly where that top rung was yet, but she dispensed with the idea of taking holy vows and started romanticising about becoming a writer. "I wrote a lot of short stories and poems ... but when I started a novel, I did about 30 pages and just stopped."

Despite the fact that her father wouldn't allow her to watch any television at home, Madonna found the focus and escapism she'd been searching for at local revival houses which screened old Hollywood movies. The flickering images fired her imagination for the first time. "I really loved them because they allowed you to fantasise. I'd watch them and think about what I wanted to be when I grew up."

During these fragile and insecure pre-teen years, Madonna looked to film stars like Grace Kelly and Bardot for inspiration, "I wanted to make my hair blonde and wear pointy bras." She fell in love with Monroe – "my first movie idol" – Carole Lombard and Judy Holliday. "They were all just incredibly funny and they were silly and sweet. I saw myself in them, my funniness and my need to boss people around, and at the same time to be taken care of. My knowingness and my innocence. Both."

In common with her heroines, Madonna wanted "to go somewhere and be somebody," and her dream of a special life found a welcome release in performing. She began by singing in school productions and church choirs. She managed to convince her father that she should take dance lessons instead of piano, and started learning ballet, baton twirling and gymnastics.

She had a brief flirtation with the prestigious role of school cheerleader and baton-twirler but found it an all-too trivial pastime. "I couldn't get into it ... it wasn't that I wasn't interested in sports, it's that I couldn't agree with the sensibilities of the athletes. They were only interested in sports, drinking and girls."

Madonna's serious, no-nonsense mentality distanced her from people of her own age and prevented her from forging any close relationships at school. "I sort of hung around on the outside of things and befriended the guys who were really studious, like physics majors."

She had a low opinion of her fellow colléagues because she felt that their sense of vision was so limited. It was as if she was moving faster than everyone around her, with such focus and vigour that the others marked her down as a misfit. "I kept myself to myself and did what I wanted to do."

Madonna concentrated on working out song and dance routines whenever she had the chance. "I bounced around and did everything. I wanted to be a movie star. And then I wanted to be a singer. Then I got into dancing and really concentrated on that."

Her school performances started earning her standing ovations, and at 12, Madonna took stock of her young life and put phase one of her world domination dream into operation. "I decided I should try and get pro about dancing." It became an all-consuming and rewarding passion. She landed lead rôles in high school productions like *My Fair Lady* and *The Sound Of Music*. Madonna was the centre of attention again.

As she grew into her teens Madonna became a fanatical Michael Jackson 'wannabe'. "I thought to myself, I can do everything he can do only I'm a girl ..."

Madonna's London début at the Camden Palace in 1983. Ironically half the guest list were no-shows.

1972/1975

At sweet 16 Madonna became a
High School rebel with a cause – to do
everything her parents told her not to do.

"When I started having a dream and working toward that goal, I finally started to really like myself for the first time." Like many teenagers, Madonna had been through one of those awkward phases of erroneous self-loathing, when "I didn't think I was beautiful or talented." But the time had come for her teenage revolution; for freedom of expression and pointy bras.

While her stepmother still found a glimpse of stocking, shocking, Madonna was determined to emulate her glamorous idols, and that meant rebelling against her parents' suffocating authority. "I wanted to do everything everybody told me I couldn't do . . . I couldn't wear make-up, I couldn't wear nylons, I couldn't cut my hair, I couldn't go on dates, I couldn't even go to the movies with my friends."

Madonna had to be home by 9.30 every night, "or there was big trouble" while her brothers were allowed to stay out late and go to concerts. "I was left out . . . somewhere deep down inside of me was a frustrated little boy."

So Madonna refused to bow to the iron rod of discipline any longer and developed a secret, double-identity. At home she appeared to play by the rules, but once she got to school she'd head straight for the ladies cloakroom and change into the glad rags of her alter ego . . . "I'd roll up my uniform skirt so it was short, I'd put make-up on and change into nylon stockings . . . and I was incredibly flirtatious."

Determined to beat the big drum of her new-found bad girl image, Madonna stopped at nothing: she wore bright, sexy knickers as her crowning glory, and made sure everyone saw them. In the playground she'd hang upside down from the monkey bars. In the classroom she'd pull her uniform over her

Madonna's early image – the rags
and tatters of a street waif.

desk top so the boys could see up her skirt. Not surprisingly, she earnt herself the reputation for being a shameless 'nympho'.

Madonna the exhibitionist knew no bounds, and delighted in shocking people. She spiced up a local talent show with an act that had her audience staring open-mouthed. "I wore a bikini and painted fluorescent flowers all over my body, and I danced under a black light with a strobe light blinking." And in 1975, when she was sweet 16, Madonna made a rather unsavoury film début when she appeared in a bizarre super-8 movie, directed by a classmate, in which an egg was fried on her stomach.

Madonna the rebel declared an act of war with her father when, one evening, she decided to ignore the consequences and sneak off to see her very first concert, David Bowie at Cobo Hall, Detroit. "Oh it was the most marvellous thing I'd ever done in my life. I was punished severely for going." At this time Madonna was also a devout worshipper of Joni Mitchell. "The 'Court And Spark' album was my Bible for a whole year. I knew every word of every song on that album."

Madonna found a soul mate, and partner in crime, when she befriended a girl who also shared the trials and tribulations of disapproving parents. "We laughed at the world together . . . we thought we were better than anybody else and our main point of interest was boys.

"We liked the floozy look because our parents didn't like it. We got dressed to the nines. We got bras and stuffed them so our breasts were over-large and wore really tight sweaters – we were sweater-girl floozies. We wore tons of lipstick and really badly applied make-up, and huge beauty marks, and we wore our hair up like the country singer Tammy Wynette."

It was a summer of unbridled madness and self discovery. Madonna started hanging out with her young uncles. "They had a rock band . . . I thought they were the coolest people in the world," and escaping to her grandmother's house in Bay City, Michigan, where she was allowed to get away with murder.

"We could eat 12 desserts at grandma's, stay out past 10.00 and go out with boys. I remember that summer I was watching my uncles' band, wearing tight jeans for the first time in my life. I smoked a cigarette, not too successfully, and I started plucking my eyebrows and feeling like, 'Yeah, this is it, I'm cool'."

Madonna had 'found' herself but lost all sense of direction. She was acting like the people she used to look down on; limiting her vision to the dizzy delights of boys, clothes and self-conceited vanity. It was a necessary detour, and one that most teenagers feel compelled to take, but Madonna's drive and self-discipline were rekindled when she befriended another girl who shared her passion for dancing.

"She looked smarter than your average girl, but in an interesting offbeat way. So I attached myself to her. She took me to ballet classes in Rochester, and that's where I met a guy called Christopher Flynn who saved me from my high school turmoil. He had his own ballet school. I really loved him."

Flynn was in his late 40's and a man of the world. He introduced Madonna to a different kind of consciousness; the world of art and culture. "I was with older and more sophisticated people. I felt really superior. I just felt that all the suffering I had gone through for not fitting in had been worth it . . . I was evolving into something else."

lynn was the first Catholic homosexual that Madonna had encountered. He was strict and disciplined – but inspiringly so. He made Madonna push herself for her own good, and he alone recognised her star quality potential. He told her she was different, special and beautiful, and they formed a mutual appreciation club.

He has said of her, "Madonna was one of the best students I ever had, she had a great deal of charisma and a sense of outrageous fun." And she has said of him, "He was my first mentor, my father, my imaginary lover, everything."

Flynn introduced Madonna to the manic pleasures of seedy gay clubs in downtown Detroit where "men were popping pills and going crazy," and he filled her head with ideas of making it big as a dancer. Madonna had finally met someone who could point the way to her special world. It wasn't in Hollywood where the streets were paved with stars – Flynn told her to brave the fast-lane frenzy of New York. "He was the one who said I could do it if I wanted to."

Madonna was initially hesitant. She had never been there before; she had no contacts there; she wasn't sure if she was ready and, naturally, her parents were against the whole crazy idea. Madonna's father urged her to study law and be respectable, while Flynn kept on encouraging her to "go for it."

But Madonna alone had to decide whether to get on out there and take a bite of the Big Apple . . .

"I think your parents give you false expectations of life. All of us grow up with completely misguided notions about life and they don't change until you get out into the world. It's like someone telling you what love or marriage is; you can't know until you're there and then you have to learn the hard way."

Madonna was anxious to get some first-hand experience of life, and prepared to learn things the hard way. One thing was for sure now, she definitely wanted to become a professional dancer.

"I finally figured out what I was going to do with my weird old self . . . I needed a skill to get out of Detroit and go to New York and I had to arm myself."

Madonna graduated from Rochester Adams High School in 1976 when she was 17, and the recognition she'd gained at her high school theatre, coupled with her strong academic achievements, won her the chance of a four-year scholarship to the University of Michigan's dance department.

But meanwhile she attended a six-week dance workshop at Duke University in Durham, North Carolina, which threw up a magnificent, chance-of-a-lifetime offer – the opportunity to dance in New York City.

Students at the Duke University workshop were invited to 'try out' for a scholarship to study with top choreographers, Alvin Ailey and Pearl Lang at Alvin Ailey's New York studio.

Hell-bent on pulling this one off, Madonna attended the auditions and marched right up to one of the judges announcing, "I'm auditioning for this school so I can work wih Pearl Lang. I saw one of her performances and she's the only one I want to work with." To which the judge replied, "I am Pearl Lang." Madonna's eyes nearly popped right out of her head.

Pearl recognised in Madonna a power and intensity that merited a place at her studio and has said of her protégée, "Madonna simply has the magical quality that a great artist needs."

Madonna had the choice of spending one brief summer in New York, or four secure years in Michigan. It was no contest . . .

"I turned down the scholarship to Michigan, and when I told my father I didn't want to go to college but wanted to go to New York and be a dancer, it didn't make any sense to him. To him, dancing was a hobby and not something you could make a living out of."

Fame, fortune and freedom seemed just a plane ride away for Madonna, and as far as she was concerned, she was moving for practical reasons too. "When I turned 17 I moved to New York because my father wouldn't let me date boys at home. I never saw a naked body when I was a kid – gosh, when I was 17 I still hadn't seen a penis!"

Her ballet teacher Christopher Flynn wished her well; her father tried to stop her, "but he couldn't put chains around my ankles . . . I left home without his blessing and I was glad to do it." She was confident that, one day, her father would come to understand and appreciate what she was doing.

Madonna packed a suitcase full of tights and dance shoes. She took 35 dollars in cash, a giant baby doll, and a picture of her real mother. With a scholarship arranged, but little else, Madonna boarded a plane for the first time in her life and set off, "to conquer the city

. . . it was the bravest thing I'd ever done."

On arrival she jumped in a cab and told the driver, "Take me to the middle of everything!" She found herself standing in Times Square looking skywards at all the tall buildings; feeling like "a small fish in a big sea," only this small fish didn't even have a place to stay for the night. She was the proverbial stranger in a strange town; all wide-eyed and gasping with excitement – and fear.

"It was a shock to me because I'd never been to a place where I didn't know anyone. When you're only 17, New York can be a very overwhelming place, nothing will ever surpass that moment for shock value."

It was a hot summer's day in New York, and Madonna looked lost and completely out of place with her suitcase and warm winter coat. She noticed a curious stranger staring intently at her, and smiled and said hello. Before long she was pouring her heart out to him, and he offered to let her stay at his apartment. Madonna naïvely took the risk. "I stayed there for the first two weeks. He didn't try to rape me or anything. He showed me where everything was and he gave me breakfast. It was perfect."

Madonna came to rely on the kindness of strangers, and any available spare couch she could find for the night, "Although I took to New York straight away I was really lonely . . . I would take whatever I could take in a taxi cab, to wherever I could go to next. I'd take a big breath, grit my teeth, blink back my tears and say, 'I'm gonna do it – I have to do it, because there's nowhere else for me to go'."

It was an awesome initiation into New York society, but Madonna lasted the course and returned home safely to Michigan when she was offered another scholarship to the University's dance department. She took it purely to fine-tune her technique, with no intention of staying any longer than she had to. "I was in the performing arts school where I studied dance, music theory, art history and a Shakespearian course.

Ballet dancers, by tradition, are supposed to be paragons of grace, poise and femininity. But, contrary as ever, Madonna went out of her way to be the exact opposite. She ripped up her tights and her leotards, and safety-pinned them back together. She cut her hair in a short spikey style, so she didn't have to wear it in a bun. She protested that it would be far more practical to dance in a bra during the hot summer months, and had the revolting habit of belching out loud in class.

"I was a real ham. I did everything I could to get attention . . . to stand out from the others and say, 'I'm not like you. OK? I'm taking dance classes and everything but I'm not stuck here'."

History was repeating itself. Just as Madonna had felt superior to everyone at high school, so she saw the students at Michigan as "bratty little girls who stared at themselves in the mirror all day." And while her health conscious classmates were catching up on their beauty sleep, Madonna danced her nights away in a local student disco called the Blue Frogge, where she finally blew her imperious cool over a black waiter called Steve Bray. "First time in my life I asked a guy to buy me a drink."

Bray was the funkiest guy Madonna had ever encountered. When he wasn't waiting tables he was drumming for a local R&B band which Madonna followed, sometimes jumping up onstage to dance with them. It was a magnetic attraction, Madonna thought Bray was "cute and soulful . . . someone you couldn't help noticing," while Bray was drawn to Madonna's beauty and the aura that surrounded her. "She stood out, her energy was really apparent."

But Bray's love couldn't tame Madonna's ambition. In 1978, after only a year at college, she broke the news that she was returning to New York – this time for good. The 19-year-old Madonna had been invited to take classes with the Alvin Ailey troupe's third company (a modest step up in the dance world) and this time it wasn't only her father who didn't want her to go. "Looking back," says Madonna, "I think that I probably did make Steve feel kind of bad, but I was really insensitive in those days. I was totally self-absorbed."

Classes with the third company were a refreshing experience. Here Madonna found herself working out with a whole bunch of self-driven, ego-orientated students. "I thought I was in a production of *Fame* . . . everyone was Hispanic or black and everyone wanted to be a star."

Life in the big city wasn't really any easier this time around, but at least now Madonna knew what to expect. Hard up as ever, she could only afford to live in a slum at 232 East Fourth Street, in New York's notorious Lower East Side. But Madonna felt an affinity with her neighbours; all the Latin and black kids who were part of the hip hop, breakdancing, graffiti-spraying street scene. She was attracted to their looks and their style, and soon became a dab hand with a spray can.

Madonna's father paid a visit to the flat to try and persuade her to return home and finish her scholarship. "He was mortified. The place was crawling with cockroaches. There were winos in the hallways and the entire place smelled of stale beer."

Madonna ignored his plea and raised the money for food and rent by slaving away in a series of fast food joints like Dunkin' Donuts, (until she was sacked for squirting jam all over the customers), Burger King, and a Greek chain called Amy's. She also worked as a coat-check girl at the stylish Russian Tea Room – until she discovered that she could exert less effort and earn more money by doing nude

Madonna reveals her new trim and toned physique for the Who's That Girl Tour.

modelling for art students.

"I started modelling for a lot of art schools, for the drawing and painting classes . . . because I was a dancer I was in really good shape, and I was slightly underweight so you could see my muscle definition and my skeleton. I was one of their favourite models because I was easy to draw."

Even so, times were still tough enough for Madonna to have to resort to garbage cans for the odd free meal, and she mostly lived on a diet of popcorn because it was "cheap, nutritious and filling."

Fortunately Madonna had been gifted with the imagination to romanticise her gypsy-like existence, and the vision to know that it was all going to lead somewhere. She wore the rags and tatters of a vagabond; picking through trashy thrift shops for weird oddments with shock-appeal; ripped up shirts, oversized men's clothes, high heeled shoes and rags for her ratted hair. "I used to be such an outgoing, crazy lass . . . I went out of my way to make

statements with my clothing and I brazenly looked people in the eye when I walked down the streets and rode the subway."

By 1979, Madonna had become a native New Yorker at heart. She had made a wealth of friends from all the would-be actors, painters and musicians who moved in the same circles as she did, and she had started dating a graffiti artist called Norris Burroughs; acknowledged to be 'the king' of the city's graffiti t-shirt designers.

The relationship only lasted for three months, and for once it was Madonna who was given the elbow. Burroughs had found a new girlfriend but, by way of compensation, he planned a little secret matchmaking between Madonna and a painter/writer/musician friend of his called Dan Gilroy. Burroughs told Madonna how wonderful Gilroy was, and vice versa, and then he threw a party and invited them both along.

Whatever expectations Gilroy had of Madonna, she more than lived up to them when she walked straight over to him and, with that upfront attitude of hers, asked "Aren't you going to kiss me?"

Gilroy's heart was all a-flutter . . . "When I kissed Madonna, it was wonderful. I melted," he coos at the memory, remembering what she was wearing right down to the last detail: "A kind of circus outfit, very short with a blue tutu, and dark blue leggings . . . and she had olive oil in her hair which made it quite strange and matted. It was influenced by punk but she was moving in her own direction.

"It was quite weird, really, because she was just kind of sitting there and she seemed depressed – I think she'd come to the party with someone she didn't want to be with. So I was her dancing partner and we hit it off and got together."

A few weeks later Madonna moved in with Dan. He lived in Corona, Queens, an area with a huge clash of cultures including Latin American, Italian, and Chinese. Dan lived with his brother Ed in an abandoned Synagogue, which doubled up as a studio. The place was full of musical instruments and Dan stuck a guitar in Madonna's hand. "He tuned it to an open chord so that I could strum. That really clicked something off in my brain . . ."

While Madonna's love life and social whirl seemed as action-packed as a hot summer's Sunday in Central Park, her dancing career had slowed down to a snail's pace. There were just too many dancers and not enough work – or money. Progression in the dance world was too limited and long-winded to hold her attention any longer, and she was sick of working her "ass off for nothing."

So Madonna thought to herself, 'Well, if you don't like it, do what you want to do. You know you can dance. You've made a lot of friends, you know musicians, so go do what you want to do . . .'

Dan (left) and Ed Gilroy – the Breakfast Club brothers.

"Once I felt really confident about my dancing I went into music. I started writing songs, but when I had to get out in front of lots of people and actually perform them, I encountered all the same fears of awkwardness and uncertainty that I felt when I first started dancing. Every time I start something new, my knees tremble, and I want to learn. I'm afraid and I'm also excited. I'm just like an open book. I want to get everything into my head that I can, then get it out . . ."

In 1979, Madonna cut back to just one dance class a day and started exploring other avenues. "I wanted to make more of my assets, you might say, so I decided to audition for the musical theatre. I'd turn up to auditions and tell them I could dance and sing, because I wanted to use my voice."

Flicking through the pages of an entertainment trade paper, an intriguing advert caught Madonna's eye. The good news was that a group of backing singers and dancers were needed for a forthcoming world tour. The bad news was that this Las Vegas style revue was fronted by a lumbering disco ham called Patrick Hernandez.

The German singer had enjoyed a huge, money-spinning international hit with a disco ditty called 'Born To Be Alive' which Madonna thought was "really horrible" but that didn't put her off auditioning.

The two portly Parisian producers in charge of proceedings, Jean Claude Pellerin and Jean Van Lieu, fell in love with Madonna's act, and asked her to return another day.

"Finally they took me in this room and said, 'We don't want you to do the revue –

we want to make you a star.' They were based in Paris and they wanted me to go there and study with a vocal coach while they found material for me. It was to be a learning situation. "They were offering me a lot of money and a recording contract. I'd never been abroad before and I wanted to see a bit of the world . . . I was in seventh heaven. I kept thinking, 'Somebody noticed me'."

Madonna and Dan Gilroy had just one month together before she had to leave for Paris. They were days of wine and roses, movies and concerts, picnics and magic. "When you know a relationship isn't meant to last," remembers Dan affectionately, "you can make each moment as intense as you want."

Dan steeled his heart and convinced himself that this short-lived relationship suited him just fine; that he didn't want any heavy involvement with Madonna and that, when the time came, it would be easy to cut the ties.

Paris was a great adventure for Madonna when she arrived; life was "like a French movie" and the romantic in her soul felt at home there, despite the usual culture shock. Madonna was a non-French speaking American in Paris so there were communication problems, but the two Jeans went out of their way to give her every possible comfort, and promised to turn her into the biggest female star in Europe. They produced several TV shows in Paris and had unlimited connections. A corny song was written for her called 'She's A Real Disco Queen', and a team of experts were brought in to groom her for megastardom.

From downtown pauper to uptown princess; Madonna found herself with a fancy apartment, a maid and a chauffeur-driven limousine. But she felt alienated by the grandeur of her luxurious surroundings, and irritated by all the spare time she had on her hands. The French producers were exceedingly generous with their money, but for Madonna, a girl's best friend was honest, hard work. She sat in her lavish apartment feeling lonely, confined and miserable, itching to get the show – any show – on the road. The Frenchmen had thought of everything – but her feelings. They had given her everything – but their time. The song they had written for Madonna remained untouched because they were too busy with other artists on their label. "I overdubbed vocals on some already-recorded disco tracks, but basically it was pretty boring."

Although Madonna couldn't speak French, it didn't take her long to work out exactly what was going on here. Her benevolent Frenchmen were using her to live out their rich man's fantasy of taking a poor little gifted girl and moulding her into a star. They wanted to create a new Edith Piaf and got their kicks from introducing Madonna to Parisian aristocrats and "Telling everybody that I was this little thing they'd found in the gutters of New York.

"Once again I was forced into the rôle of *enfant terrible*. All I wanted to do was make trouble because they stuck me in an environment that didn't allow me to be free."

When they gave Madonna money to go out and buy glamorous 'disco' clothes, she came back with black boots, black jeans, and a black leather jacket. "And I had my ears pierced and put safety pins in them." When they took her to expensive restaurants, she'd deliberately show them up by sitting down and ordering three desserts.

Madonna fled her gilded cage and befriended the only Parisians she could identify with: the Algerian and Vietnamese young guns who spent their days driving around the city on motorcycles, terrorising people. "I've always been attracted to people like that because they're irresponsible and they challenge the norm. I try to rehabilitate them. I guess I'm just trying to be the mother I never had."

Madonna went clubbing with the locals and managed to get to Tunisia with the Hernandez tour. Back home in New York, Dan Gilroy missed Madonna more than he ever imagined and put pen to paper. "He was my saving grace, his letters were so funny. He'd paint a picture of an American flag and write over it, like it was from the President, 'We miss you. You must return to America'." However far away, Dan was the one person that made Madonna feel wanted – and homesick.

For anyone else, it would have been a tough decision to return to New York and start all over again. But not for Madonna. "I believe that you can't have lasting happiness unless you've actually worked hard for your reward." By her standards, the French producers were strictly in the glass slipper business. Her dancing had won her a trip to Paris and all the money she could spend, but Madonna wasn't yet a material girl. Fame was her priority, not fortune, and if that meant returning to the gutter then so be it.

Madonna was ready to turn her back on Paris when she had the misfortune to contract a severe bout of pneumonia, but as soon as she was well enough to travel, she told the Frenchmen that she needed a holiday, and left for good.

"I hadn't signed any contracts so I just left everything I had there and never returned . . . as far as actual productive musical stuff, I had nothing to show for the six months I had spent there."

But the one thing Paris had given Madonna was plenty of time to think seriously about which direction she should be taking her career. "By the time I got to New York I had so much pent-up energy, I knew for sure that I wanted to be a singer."

Madonna spent the next few months crashing at an illustrator friend's place, and spending every day with Dan Gilroy. She told him she'd been smitten with the music bug and Dan was prepared to help by teaching her everything he knew.

Dan had a theory that anybody with a sense of timing could be a drummer, so that was to be Madonna's starting point. "Being a dancer certainly helped me learn how to play instruments . . . when you're playing on the drums, it's all about being co-ordinated."

While Dan went to work every day, Madonna had the run of his studio. "I became an excellent drummer. I was really strong and I'd had all this dance training so I had all this energy. Instead of dancing eight hours a day, I was practising the drums for four hours a day – I drove everybody mad!"

Dan taught Madonna how to play chord progressions and she started teaching herself guitar. Despite her childhood loathing for piano lessons, she even started tinkling at the ivories again, and experimenting with keyboards. "It was an intensive musical training, but I was full of energy and raring to go."

Once she had enough musical knowledge to start writing her own songs, Madonna would wait for Dan to come home and use him as her sounding board. Dan was an emotional lump at heart and, "Sometimes I'd write sad songs and he'd sit there and cry . . . it was very sweet."

It was early 1980, Madonna was 20 and she had never felt so happy or so loved in all her life. Her relationship with Dan was fulfilling in many ways; he was her best friend, her lover and her music teacher. "I stayed at Dan and Ed's studio so much, but I hadn't actually moved in there, so one day I said, 'Can I just live here, Dan?' and he said, 'Well, we'll have to ask Ed,' and I said, 'Ed – you have to ask Ed!'"

Not only did Madonna manage to persuade the Gilroy brothers into letting her take up permanant residence at their synagogue, she also persuaded them into letting her join their band – along with a fellow ex-dancer friend of hers called Angie Smit.

And then there were four . . . they called themselves The Breakfast Club because rehearsals invariably didn't finish until the early hours of the morning, when they would trot over to the local pancake house and order buckwheats for breakfast.

Never one to do anything half-heartedly, Madonna put one hundred per cent effort into The Breakfast Club, and expected the others to do the same. "She was a maniac for rehearsing," says Dan. "Rehearse, rehearse, rehearse – she was a real workaholic."

She had become obsessional about the group. Thinking big was second nature to Madonna, and in her mind's eye The Breakfast Club were gigging, signing deals and recording. Now all she had to do was to make it happen.

"She'd be up in the morning," remembers Dan. "She'd have a quick cup of coffee and then sit by the phone and call up everybody – everyone from local record dealers to potential management."

But Madonna was now guilty of having only her own interests at heart. Just like the time she had left her Michigan boyfriend, Steve Bray, to take up dancing in New York, she was becoming increasingly self-absorbed. "I took advantage of the situation," she admits. "I wanted to know everything they knew because I knew I could make it work to my benefit."

After several months of rehearsals, The Breakfast Club played "all the Lower East Side hellholes in New York." Madonna took the back seat playing drums, "But I was always thinking, 'I want to be a singer in this group too.' And they didn't need another singer."

Nevertheless, Madonna made a bid for the spotlight and after "having begged for ages" Dan agreed to write her a couple of songs which she could perform in the act.

The first time Madonna stepped out from behind her drum kit and moved to centre stage, she felt a little shaky and unsure. Dancing she could do; drumming she could do; but here was another new experience. A familiar combination of fear and excitement swept through her body as Madonna belted out her songs for all she was worth, drawing strength from her two musical heroines, Chrissie Hynde and Debbie Harry.

"Chrissie Hynde from The Pretenders was a great musical inspiration to me at that time. I thought she had a great voice, she was gutsy and she was a great musician. I also admired Debbie Harry. I was just starting to write music when she was popular. They were both inspiring because they were women and they were in charge of what they were

doing. They were obviously writing their own lyrics and they had very strong images. They gave me courage."

By the end of the evening Madonna was hooked on singing, and The Breakfast Club had mutated into a two-headed monster. Dan and Ed had already asked Angie Smit to leave the band because her ridiculously skimpy costumes had detracted from the music. Now Madonna was competing for the spotlight and

Dan's loyalties were torn between her, and his brother Ed.

Madonna had no such problem. She knew that her priority had to be her career, and after a year with The Breakfast Club she decided to move back to Manhattan and form her own band. "I knew that Dan and Ed were afraid that I was going to steal all the attention, so I thought to myself, 'I'm going to have to leave and front my own band'."

The good times had come to an end, and Dan felt an emptiness that he hadn't felt since Madonna left the last time, for Paris. "I missed her very much. It had been a good year. Having Madonna there had been a bonus."

It would have been easy for Dan to feel bitter and exploited, but he realised that someone with Madonna's drive and devotion had to be a free spirit, and it was a feeling he understood.

"There was the normal separation anxiety of course," says Dan, "But I think we both knew our relationship didn't have a feeling of permanency in it."

Madonna moved into a draughty old loft and began recruiting musicians. She thought of calling her group Modern Dance or The Millionaires but, in memory of Dan Gilroy, Madonna settled on Emmy, after the nickname he had given her when she was a fully-fledged member of The Breakfast Club.

At last it seemed Madonna could have it all her own way, and she nominated herself as lead singer and guitarist. But it didn't take long for her to realise she was kingpin of a motley crew, who were completely out of control. The band she'd hired were nothing more than a bunch of second-class mercenaries who would leave at the first sniff of failure, and Madonna was too much of a novice to throw her weight around and tell them how to play.

Alone in a wilderness of incompetent musicians, she needed a new ally to help pull everything magically into shape. To her surprise, she found an old one. Her Michigan boyfriend Steve Bray got in touch with the news that he was thinking of moving to New York to try his hand as a drummer. She invited him to join Emmy, and despite past differences, Bray promised he'd be right by her side at the end of the week. Madonna wiped the sweat off her brow and began to believe in miracles. Someone up there was looking after her and "Steve Bray was a lifesaver."

They wrote music together on his little home studio and booked Emmy into the usual run down, low life New York clubs. If they were lucky they got $25 a gig. Money was short, and one by one the band walked out. Only Bray remained loyal.

Madonna and Bray had a budget plan: one dollar a day for food which they spent on yoghurt and peanuts in the local Korean delicatessens. And there were always garbage cans. "If there was a Burger King bag sitting on top that someone had just deposited, I'd open it up and if I was lucky there'd be some French fries that hadn't been eaten – I'm vegetarian."

Accommodation became an added problem when Madonna's loft caught fire. She was sleeping on the floor surrounded by electric heaters, when she woke up to find the carpet in flames. "I jumped up and dumped water everywhere, which only made it spread more. Then my nightgown caught fire." She whipped it off, grabbed her clothes and ran.

adonna eventually whipped off all her clothes in an effort to survive and fund the band. She decided to take up nude modelling again. "I started modelling privately for people who had little get-togethers on weekends, so I got to know the artists in a friendly kind of way. They became like surrogate mothers and fathers and they took care of me.

"Eventually they started recommending me to photographers who were doing exhibits on nudes, and photography sessions paid more than drawing." Madonna didn't feel this work entered the realms of pornography, and considered the nude "a work of art." She closed her eyes, thought of Michelangelo, and kept saying to herself, "It's for art."

Many a would-be star has fallen into the trap of baring their all for the camera in moments of despair and impatience. For their sins, and the fat bounty cheques waved by soft porn magazines, these pictures are sure to surface if the would-be star makes it big. Madonna, however, didn't stop to think at the time that this could ever happen to her because "the pictures were never meant for publication," and she couldn't yet imagine herself becoming famous enough to merit that kind of voyeuristic attention.

Through her contacts, Madonna also became involved in some 16 millimetre art movies. "They had no story, they were just images chopped up to make you 'think' about things. I was doing all sorts of wacky things, screaming and running around changing costumes, and having monologues with myself talking to the camera."

Acting had, of course, always been on Madonna's list of aspirations, so when she saw an advert in a paper announcing auditions for a lead part in what looked like a big league art movie, she applied. She didn't have the usual glossy photo and resumé that professional actresses send out, so she went for a completely different approach. She sent the director/writer a two-page handwritten letter giving her life story, along with a photo of herself sitting on a bus applying bright red lipstick with her finger.

The film was being made by a young man in his final year at the New York University Film School, Stephen Jon Lewicki. Her alternative approach appealed to him and his manner of auditioning was equally bizarre. He invited Madonna to meet him for a tête-à-tête in Washington Square Park, where she made her usual, devastating impact. Lewicki was instantly smitten. "She had a riveting personality. She had the charisma that makes a star a star." He told Madonna she was perfect for the lead rôle in his avant-garde underground film, A Certain Sacrifice which turned out to be little more than a low budget soft porn movie, for which Madonna would be paid the sum of $100. At the time she wanted the acting experience and managed to convince herself that the whole sorry sado-masochistic plot was just, "Real stupid and hilarious." But when she was honest with herself she had to admit it was actually "very sick."   "It was sick in a childish kind of way. It's about this girl in post punk New York called Bruna, who's a dominatrix – me of course. There's hardly any sex scenes, it's just implied all the time. She's got love slaves and she leads this really perverted, deranged life. I get raped, which you don't see in the movie, and my boyfriend goes crazy with revenge, kills the guy and performs this ritual sacrifice. There's a scene where we take a bath in fake blood."

Lewicki developed a serious crush on Madonna during the making of the film, and claims to have eaten blueberry yoghurt out of her ear one crazy day in Battery Park. "That woman," he concluded, "has more sensuality in her ear than most women have got anywhere in their bodies."

The promo poster for the rather unsavoury A Certain Sacrifice art movie.

Madonna with some of her New
York graffiti gang chums.

He also praised her for her
professionalism. "She is the consummate
professional; on time, understands her role,
and always delivers her lines. But he found her
a complex character to deal with. "She has a
tremendous need for approval . . . and an
incredible swing of moods in her personal life.
She can express deep love, then fiery hatred
for the same thing or person within a few
minutes."

I n 1981, between filming and writing
new songs, Madonna and Bray
rented rehearsal space at a rock 'n'
roll haunt called The Music Buildings; 12 floors
of rehearsal rooms in a decaying high rise
where the so-called cream of New York's
music scene lived and laboured. Madonna and
Bray joined the communal set-up and slept
among the amplifiers.

For most of the bands there
success meant procuring a regular gig at one of
New York's happening nightclubs – and there
the dream ended. For Madonna to waltz in
with her high-faluting ideas of nationwide hits
was an insult to their cool. The others frowned
on her, but it was a mutual loathing. "I thought
they were all lazy," says Madonna. "I thought
that only a handful of people were going to get
out of that building to any success."

"There was a lot of resentment of
someone who's obviously got that special

something," remembers Bray. "She had trouble
making friends."

Madonna and Bray recruited
another band and Emmy developed into a
hard-rocking outfit, with Madonna belting out
songs up front. Things were looking up
musically, with one major drawback; they
couldn't find a competent guitarist for love nor
money, and without one, the sound didn't gel.
Madonna wanted to change their name from
Emmy to Madonna and "Steve thought that
was disgusting," but the whole matter was of
no consequence, since lack of money had
driven everyone away again.

Madonna's life seemed to be
developing a distinct cyclic pattern. Whenever
things looked as if they just couldn't get any
worse, a miracle would come to pass and
everything turned around. In the autumn of
1981 she and Bray were just about due for
one. As luck would have it, Madonna spotted a
guy getting out of the lift in the Music Buildings
and, with her usual flirtatious panache, yelled
out, "Hey, you look like John Lennon!" His
name was Adam Alter, and when they got
talking she discovered that he, and a woman
called Camille Barbone, had just formed a rock
management company called Gotham
Productions. They had a rehearsal studio and
they were looking for acts to manage and
produce.

Adam Alter and Camille Barbone
listened to her demo tape and agreed that
"Madonna was destined for great things . . . to

say we believed in her is an understatement."
Camille agreed to manage Madonna, and they
became firm friends. They found that, oddly
enough, they shared the same birthday;
Camille was exactly eight years older than the
22-year-old Madonna, and she became
another of those 'surrogate mothers'. "I
discovered that she didn't have any money and
hadn't eaten for three days," remembers
Camille. "She had a guitar, but the neck was
broken. She had a bicycle, but that had a flat
tyre . . . I felt sorry for her, she was really in
need."

Madonna's needs were emotional
as well. She had become seriously
involved with a painter called Kenny
Compton who was two-timing her, and
Camille was a good listener and shoulder to cry
on. The advice and help Camille offered
stretched far beyond the bounds of duty – but
she was setting herself up for a fall.

When Madonna signed to Gotham
Management she was moved into spacious digs
in a safe and roomy Upper West Side
apartment. She was given free licence to use
The Gotham Studio, musicians and rehearsal
space were paid for by her management, and
she was put on a salary of $100 a week.
Despite protests from Gotham, she insisted
that Bray remain as her drummer. She also
insisted that her band change its name to
Madonna. How could Bray refuse?

Camille and Madonna grew very
close, too close, for Camille let her maternal
urges run away with her. She was living her life
through Madonna, and losing sight of her own.
Madonna's happiness was her prime, and
obsessional, concern. "I wanted to be the best
manager in the world," gushes Camille.
"I became Madonna and Madonna became me.
If I could sing in another time and place,
Madonna would have managed me. It's hard to
talk about her and not sound in love with her.
I guess I did love Madonna. I gave her
everything . . ."

Camille raved about Madonna to
her contacts and pumped her head full of great
expectations; then wondered why the humble,
modest girl she'd first encountered was
distancing herself, and cocking a snook at her
generosity. Adam Alter was really worried
about things getting out of hand.

"Camille inflated Madonna's head
with the star thing in a way that was
unbelievable," he said. Madonna concedes that

her renewed confidence triggered her haughty streak. "I can be arrogant sometimes, but I never mean it intentionally . . . I always acted like a star long before I was one."

The Gotham relationship soured, and Camille became possessed of a devilish rage when she realised, rather belatedly, that no one was in charge of Madonna's destiny but Madonna herself.

It was a fact of life with Madonna that Dan Gilroy had grown to accept when he said, "I think a lot of people feel exploited by Madonna, but then again everyone's got so many expectations about a relationship with her. She's very intense immediately with somebody, very friendly. Then, if there is any cooling of that, it's taken to be rejection."

Bray understood her too. "If people felt exploited by Madonna – that's resentment of someone who's got drive. It seems like you're leaving people behind or you're stepping on them, and the fact is that you're moving and they're not . . . Madonna doesn't care if she ruffles someone's feathers."

Camille exacted revenge with sticks and stones, and some very hurtful words. "I made her cry. I screamed at her and told her that she was a manipulative egomaniac who didn't give a damn about anyone . . . She once provoked me to such a state of anger that I bashed my fists through a door and broke my wrist." Camille had backed herself into a bitter corner, where she seethed and licked her wounds and hatched plans to get her own back – one day. When the time was right.

Some of the entrants for a Madonna lookalike held by the pop programme *The Tube*.

Meanwhile, Madonna and Bray forged ahead writing new material and Gotham booked the band into clubs where they rocked the house with a style of music influenced by one of Madonna's favourite bands, The Pretenders.

Adam Alter acknowledged that Madonna's creative strength went hand in hand with her passionate Latin temperament. "Like most good artists she is very emotional. When she's sad or in a bad mood, she can't do anything. But get her in the right circumstances and she sets the studio on fire ... that girl can write, sing and perform hits."

It was 1982 and Madonna was a hot property. Her band had cultivated a following and the buzz was reaching out to people that mattered. Record company talent scouts turned up to see what all the fuss was about and liked what they saw, but Gotham Management failed to conclude a contract. Their funds were running low, time was running out and tempers were exceedingly frayed. What's more, Madonna was having a musical change of heart.

She and Bray often spent their nights doing the disco rounds, and discovered that the city was alive with the sound of funk. Funk was the sound on the dancefloor, the sound on New York's hippest radio stations, and it was belting out from ghetto blasters in streets all over town. Disco funk groups like Shalamar caused Madonna to have a serious rethink about her musical style, and she was attracted by the British electronic dance music now beginning to make an impact on America.

"I've always been into rhythmic music, party music, but Gotham weren't used to that stuff, and although I'd agreed to do rock and roll, my heart was no longer in it. Soul was my main influence and I wanted my sound to be the kind of music I'd always liked. I wanted to approach it from a very simple point of view because I wasn't an incredible musician. I wanted it to be direct.

"I still loved to dance and all I wanted to do was make a record that I would want to dance to, and people would want to listen to on the radio."

Madonna and Bray put a funkier edge on their new material and Gotham disapproved, moaning that since they were the ones who had gone broke promoting Madonna, they were entitled to artistic control. But after a year of being pushed around and getting nowhere, Madonna decided the time had come to quit. "Finally I said, 'Forget it, I can't do this any more. I'm going to have to start all over'." It was time to return to the gutter – yet again.

If there was one thing Madonna was good at, it was knowing when to cut her losses and run. She had sought fame in New York for five hectic years now, in one form or another, and she'd come close a few times. But money couldn't buy her, and empty promises didn't impress her. She just kept moving on . . .

"I lost everything. My demo tape was the property of Gotham Management, I was living back on the street and sleeping in studios, and I'd have to walk around in the same clothes for weeks. But I'm very resilient.

"All I could do was get a new demo tape together and try to get a record deal. Steve was good at getting keys for studios after midnight because he started working as a musician for a lot of people. We'd sneak in and make tapes."

Madonna and Bray worked around the clock and wrote four new songs together: 'Everybody', 'Burning Up', 'Stay' and 'Ain't No Big Deal'. Realising they still didn't know enough about the music business to get by without a little help from some contacts, Madonna went exploring. She knew a good place to start was the DJ booths in clubs where influential people hung out.

Madonna hit the dance floor in her distinctive rags; she knew how to look a million on a few dollars, and set her own personal style with ripped up net tops and stockings, distressed knitwear and lingerie, and lashings of metal and rubber jewellery which she got from a French designer friend called Maripol. Everyone who went to the clubs wanted to make 'something' of themselves – she was in good company.

N ew York's official home for aspiring young hipsters was the Danceteria disco, where DJ Mark Kamins was king of the turntables. Kamins, an ex-A&R man turned dance-mix producer, had record company connections. He had just finished producing an album for Capitol, and was on the look out for more record deals to produce.

Madonna, with her ever-naked bellybutton, didn't have to make much of an effort to catch Kamins' beady eye. "There was a crowd out there that came every Saturday night to dance," remembers Kamins. "Madonna was special, she had her own style and a tremendous desire to perform for people. When she started tearing up the dance floor, there'd be 20 people getting up and dancing with her. She was innocent, ambitious, broke and confused. She was living a hard life."

Kamins and Madonna flirted with one other, then started dating and going to clubs together. She gave him a copy of her funk demo. "The next day he played it over the speakers before the club opened and said,

'God, this is good – I'm going to get you a record deal'."

Kamins was keen to work with Madonna. He took her into the studio to knock her tape into shape, and contacted a young and rising talent scout he knew called Michael Rosenblatt. Rosenblatt worked for Sire Records, the new wave rock label distributed by Warner Brothers. He was a good choice to approach, and suddenly, after all the waiting, all the false starts, hiccups and new beginnings, things began to take off for Madonna – at the speed of light.

Rosenblatt agreed to meet Madonna in the club one night. He had no idea what she looked like, but when he saw "an incredibly wild-looking and beautiful girl" making an entrance, he went straight over and introduced himself. A week later, Madonna and Kamins took their tape to his office, and an hour later, they had all agreed to a record deal.

But the ball couldn't roll officially, until the President of Sire Records gave his approval, and Seymour Stein was laid up in Lenox Hill Hospital with heart trouble. Nevertheless, Rosenblatt rushed to his bedside to play him the tape. "The minute I heard it," Stein remembers enthusiastically, "I knew she was special, so I called her up and asked her to come and see me next day."

At the time, Madonna had never heard of Seymour Stein, but he was, and is, acknowledged as one of America's great record company moguls. An eccentric music buff with a visionary ear for big acts and the conviction to follow his instincts, he is not the type to sign a pretty girl just because she has a 'certain something'; Madonna had yet to convince him that she had genuine talent too.

She didn't know what to expect from the strange meeting that followed. "I had this idea that I was going to meet some really cold sort of person in a suit and tie," she said. But Seymour Stein was full of expectations. "You know, you normally don't care what you

look like when you're in hospital. But I shaved, I combed my hair. I even got a new dressing gown. From what I'd heard, I was excited to meet Madonna."

T he next day, Madonna, Kamins and Rosenblatt set off to the hospital. But Stein had forgotten to wear that new dressing gown. "Here was this guy sitting there in his boxer shorts with a drip feed in his arm and goofing around." Madonna laughs at the memory. "He had a big ghetto blaster sitting on the window sill. He played my songs, right while I was there, in front of me, and he was raving, 'It's great! It's great!', talking a mile a minute. I thought the guy was nuts, but he liked my music, so I wasn't going to complain."

Stein did indeed go mental when he met Madonna in the flesh and played that tape again. "I knew I just sensed that there was something that set her apart. She was outgoing, strong, dynamic, and self assured. I just wanted to rush right in and do a deal." He signed her immediately to make three 12-inch dance singles and offered her an advance of $5000.

It wasn't the biggest record deal in the history of music, but it was a genuine offer. Madonna thought, 'What have I got to lose?' and agreed. She had just signed to the label whose roster included one of her favourite stars; Chrissie Hynde from The Pretenders.

Seymour Stein, President of Sire Records, who gave Madonna her first break.

6

DISCO NIGHTS

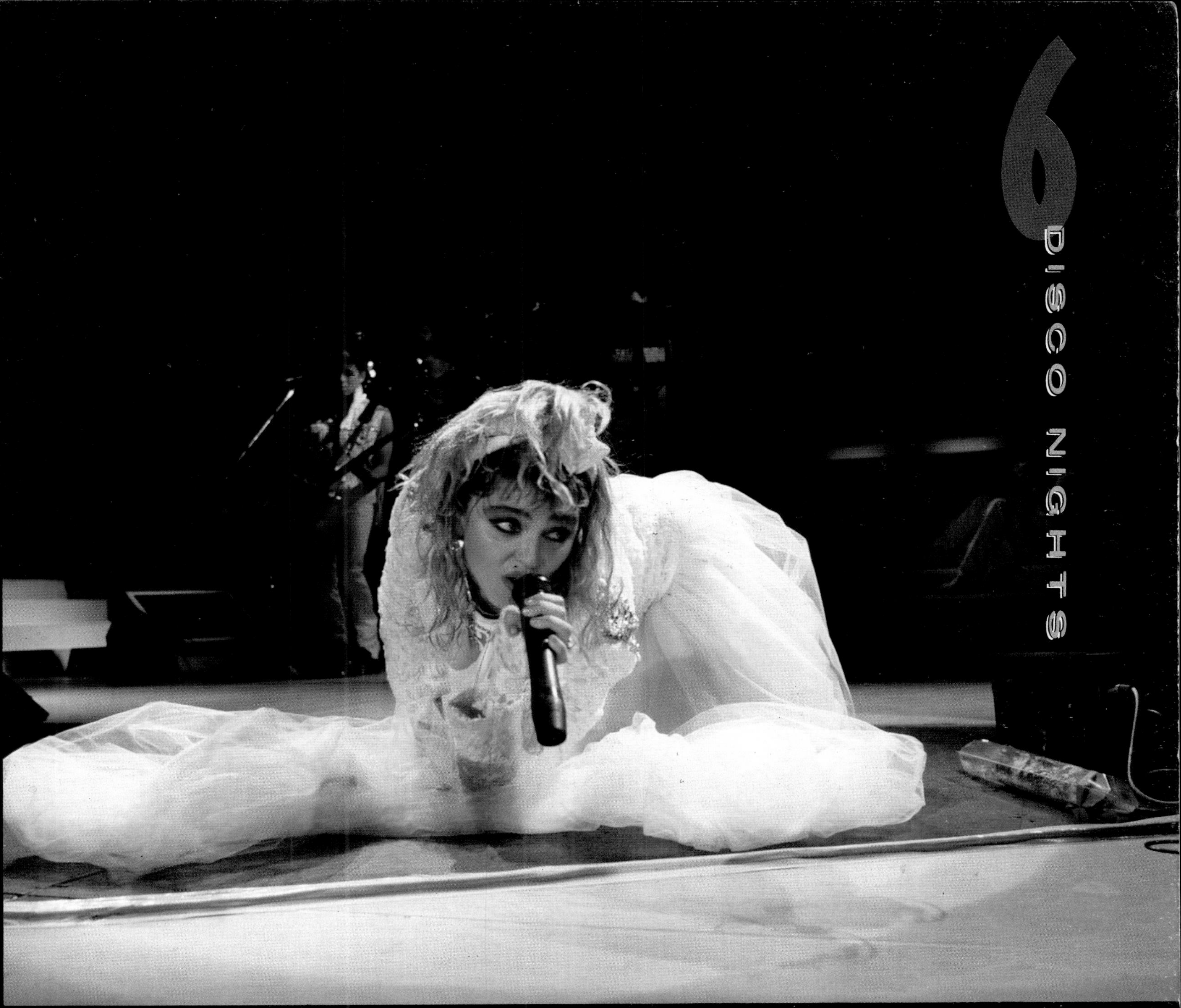

"An image and a good hook can get you in the door, but something has to keep you in the room." **Madonna.**

Everyone was happy. Sire had signed Madonna, Madonna was going to make her first single, and Kamins was going to produce it as his reward for helping to secure the deal. Rosenblatt called the tune as to which track would be released and chose 'Ain't No Big Deal' with 'Everybody' as the B-side.

But in the spring of 1982, when the two cuts were made in the studio, it was 'Everybody' that proved to be the worthier A-side, and it ended up on both sides of the single.

Appropriately, Madonna showcased her song with a performance at the Danceteria. She was merely asked to turn up and mime over a backing tape, but with her dance training in mind, she decided to "make something more visual out of it," and roped in three dancers to back up her act. One of these was Martin Burgoyne, the gay illustrator friend who had let her crash at his flat when she returned, homeless, from her Paris escapade. Madonna had also decided to involve him with the design of her record sleeves.

Rosenblatt and Stein were in the audience as Madonna walked on stage and she intended to do far more than simply promote her single. Her real ambition was to convince Sire that she was worth more than a three single record deal, and the audience at Danceteria supported her cause by going wild as she began to belt: 'I've been watching you . . . yeah . . . hurrh . . . I know you wanna get up . . .'

'Everybody' met with clubland approval but because of the American chart system of pigeon-holing musical styles into so many different, and conflicting categories dance versus pop; black versus white; AOR versus new wave, there was a great deal of confusion over how to tag Madonna's music. She saw it as "pop with a definite R&B sound," others hailed her as the first new wave disco artist, and the black radio programmers assumed she was a black singer because her sweet, white voice had so much soul – a tribute to the girl who had always been a Motown fan.

No picture of Madonna appeared on her record sleeve and many believed her to be black for some time, a misconception that suited Sire and saw the single skipping up the dance and R&B charts, making a slight impact on the pop charts, and shifting about 80,000 copies in total. "When people saw me they were real surprised that I was white," remembers Madonna. "But it didn't bother me. I just had to laugh about it."

As the single grew in popularity Madonna was invited to do more and more 'track dates' in discos, and it also amused her that, after so many years of playing live for a pittance, she was being rewarded more handsomely for miming. "The whole concept was completely new to me – it didn't make sense," she said.

With the release of her second single 'Burning Up'and the gradual realisation that she was actually a white artist, there were airplay problems in some areas. "It offended radio programmers in the South; it seemed like reverse racism but I could understand it, because MTV seemed prejudiced against black groups. The British charts are so much healthier because everything crosses over ... Warners just didn't know how to push me. I didn't fit into any category, I wanted to start a new one."

A low budget club video was made to help promote 'Burning Up' in which Madonna's on-and-off boyfriend Kenny Compton played the part of a driver who was trying to run her down. Ironically, he then turned around and laid the news on her that, after a relationship which had lasted for over two years, he never wanted to see her again. "It was the longest monogamous relationship I'd had at the time," says Madonna; monogamous on her part that was.

But Madonna had just befriended the in-house DJ at the Funhouse disco called John Benitez, a Catholic guy from the South Bronx whom everyone referred to by his nickname, 'Jellybean'. "She was introduced to me by her record company," remembers Jellybean. "I thought she had a lot of style, and she crossed over a lot of boundaries 'cos everyone in the rock clubs played her, the black clubs, the gay, the straight; and very few records have that appeal."

Madonna arriving at
Los Angeles Airport.

either the recently jilted Madonna nor the up-and-coming Jellybean felt the earth move when they first laid eyes on each other. "He took me round to all the DJs in the major clubs; places that were playing my records," remembers Madonna. "He liked me, but nothing really happened in the beginning. We were both a bit cool."

"She didn't bowl me over at first," says Jellybean. "We just used to go to the movies and clubs together, then we started holding hands and buying each other presents."

The new friendship was a timely one for the mutually ambitious couple; Madonna's huge following in the discos had finally convinced Sire to kick off 1983 by starting work on a new single and début album. They were now prepared to start ploughing big money into promoting her as a pop artist.

Money was still tight for Madonna despite her initial success and she moved into a digustingly smelly rooming house frequented by junkies. No-one liked visiting her there, but its saving grace was that it overlooked the prestigious Madison Square Garden where America's most popular rock musicians played, and Madonna consoled herself with the view from her window, and the dream that she would play there herself one day.

Madonna's début album became an object of controversy when both Steve Bray and Mark Kamins felt they had the right to produce it, even though they were relatively inexperienced for such a task. It was a tricky situation; the two ex-boyfriends had played an integral part in the first few chapters of Madonna's success story; but she felt there would be no happy ending – for any of them – unless this album had a professional producer at the helm to push her voice, and her songs, to the limit.

Madonna and her new love, DJ John 'Jellybean' Benitez.

She had the unenviable task of breaking the news to the loyal Bray first. "I was really scared. I felt I had been given a golden egg with this album and I just didn't trust Steve enough to produce it. I said he could play the instruments, but he didn't believe in the ethics of the situation . . . it was really awful."

"It was very hard to accept at the time," remembers Bray. It was his turn to have his feathers ruffled by Madonna; his turn to resent her for her ability to move on; a quality he had always defended in the old days. He walked out on her to join a band which had been going for some time – Dan Gilroy's Breakfast Club.

Next Kamins had to be told that Madonna's golden egg was far too fragile for him to cut his teeth on. "Sure, I was hurt," he acknowledges. "I felt stepped on because it was always understood that I would produce her, but later I realised she was making the right career move." Kamins admits that his time with Madonna gave his own career a boost; he had gained valuable experience and credibility.

"Madonna manipulates her own way but I don't think there's a mean bone in her body. Maybe a knuckle or two . . . "

Madonna's tough but professional decision had cost her two of her best friends. "I felt guilty because I felt like I was travelling through people. But I think that's true of most ambitious, driven people. You take what you can, then move on. If the people can't move with you – whether it's a physical or emotional move – I feel sad about that. That's part of the tragedy of love."

The professional producer hired to engineer Madonna's golden egg was Reggie Lucas, who had a sound reputation in the business for working with female vocalists like Roberta Flack and Stephanie Mills. A cast of classy session musicians was hired to play on the sessions; people who had worked with soul legends like Luther Vandross and Aretha Franklin.

While pre-production was in

progress, Sire sent Madonna across the Atlantic to try and break 'Everybody' in England, where it had only just been released. It was a daunting task. She played London's trendiest club, The Camden Palace, but half the guest list were no-shows. On a former visit to the Palace in 1981, Madonna had made the acquaintance of a strange young regular called Boy George. "I remember he came over with these big high heels on and a whole entourage of people dressed like him. He kept going on about this group he had, but I wouldn't believe him." Now Boy George was a mega-star – but Madonna still had a long way to go to prove herself in England.

Back in America, Madonna asked Jellybean to advise on the mixing of her album and three songs, 'Burning Up', 'Lucky Star' and 'Physical Attraction', got the Jellybean dance-mix treatment. As the sessions neared completion and the ill-fated dance track, 'Ain't No Big Deal', again failed to come up to expectations, the hunt was on for a suitable replacement.

It just so happened that Jellybean had a demo tape of a catchy disco song written by a couple called Curtis Hudson and Lisa Stevens. The song was called 'Holiday' and Madonna loved it. She asked Jellybean to produce it for her and as they worked closely together, the studio started exploding with an obvious hit. Their creative chemistry made 'Holiday' leap out as the best track on the album. And the emotional chemistry had finally made the earth move too . . . "He turned into my producer and my boyfriend," says Madonna. "Everything happened at the same time. We were both very ambitious and we both wanted to be stars."

'Holiday' was the obvious lead-off single for the album, and was released in June with high hopes that it would steam into the pop charts as an American summer anthem. To everyone's bewildered disappointment, it was only a modest success. "But I thought to myself, 'I know this record is good and one of these days Warner Brothers and the rest of them are going to figure it out'."

To make matters worse, Madonna wasn't too enamoured of Reggie Lucas' efforts as producer for her début album. She approved of the fact that it was "a totally aerobics record," but the sound was too slick for her liking. Madonna preferred a more sparse sound but had lacked the confidence to speak out at the time because she felt she still had much to learn. "I wanted a sound that was mine, and it wasn't until the album was nearly finished that I thought, 'Hey I know a lot more about this than I'm giving myself credit for'."

Madonna now decided to enlist the aid of a proper manager to administer her career. She still idolised Michael Jackson above any other performer because he was doing exactly what she wanted to do. "He transcended almost every level and appealed to everyone, and he had conquered the world. I thought, 'I want his manager'."

Madonna flew to Los Angeles to meet the great Freddie De Mann and he agreed to come to New York to see her play. "He came to see a show I did at Studio 54 and I was so nervous because Michael Jackson's so incredible live and I thought, 'If he thinks Prince is terrible', which he did, 'what can I do?' But he liked the show." Freddie paid Madonna the ultimate compliment by declaring, "She will be a female Michael Jackson." He also said he would manage her.

Meanwhile in England, the British public failed to respond to the records that were being released, the 'Madonna' album, and the singles 'Lucky Star' and 'Holiday. But back in America, as summer gave way to winter, 'Holiday' belatedly turned into a miraculous, marvellous Top 20 Christmas hit.

Madonna remembers her rather down-to-earth reaction at the time. "It had been hard making it as a woman. I had worked my butt off to get to this point; literally starved and lived on the street, so when it finally happened I thought to myself: 'You deserve it'." She celebrated by treating herself to her very first colour TV with a VHS machine and a push-button remote control.

With 'Holiday in the charts Madonna became an instant household name in the States, but it was a name that very few could fit a face or an image to. She had still had no video exposure on MTV, but Madonna was already thinking on an even larger scale. She had reactivated her big-screen dreams of movie stardom and started studying acting with coach Mira Rostova, whose 'Method' style made Marlon Brando famous.

"Music was still very important to me, but I had always had a great interest in films, and the thought that I could only make records for the rest of my life filled me with horror." Just as Madonna believed that she could cross over musical boundaries, she also held the conviction that she could mix her careers. "Judy Garland did it I thought, and 'If actress Sissy Spacek can be a country singer, then why can't I be an actress?' I didn't see it as being so diverse. After you've done an album you often have to wait around for six months while it's promoted, so I thought I might as well act in that time."

Madonna signed to agent William Morris and auditioned for several movies. One of those films was *Footloose* but Madonna was turned down. Another was a Jon Peters production called *Visionquest*. "It was a coming-of-age movie about a guy who's training for the Olympics. In the end he wins his big fight but loses his girl . . . I was offered a small part as a night club singer and asked to do three songs for the soundtrack

Madonna, burning up
on the dance floor.

which was being scored by Phil (*Flashdance*) Ramone. It wasn't exactly an acting role, but it was a bona fide movie, and it was an invaluable foot in the door."

In between filming for *Visionquest*, Madonna and Jellybean moved into a converted warehouse loft in fashionable Soho in downtown Manhattan. "It was huge, 2,000 square feet, with wooden floors and windows on every wall. We had a bed, a table overlooking the street and lots of mirrors for

my choreography. All the artists lived there, David Byrne from Talking Heads was a neighbour." Madonna and Jellybean were besotted with each other. They were both as "goal orientated" as each other, and their careers were exploding with the same intensity. Madonna hadn't been home to see her father Sylvio for two years and at Thanksgiving, with her hit single 'Holiday' doing so well, the prodigal daughter returned and introduced Jellybean to the family. "The last

time I'd been home I was starving and they all went, 'You are disgusting'. But now they'd heard my record on the radio and I figured my father would finally be convinced that going to the University Of Michigan was not the only alternative for me."

He was – sort of. "He was quite proud of me, though he didn't approve of it all." One thing he must have approved of was the dedication on Madonna's début album – to Sylvio Ciccone.

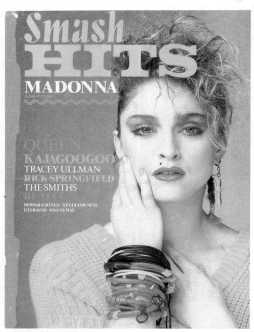

Who's that girl indeed? A new face appears on the cover of *Smash Hits*.

Madonna as a jailbird in *Who's That Girl*.

In 1984, Madonna returned to Britain to try to muster some interest in 'Holiday' which had been floating around there since November. This time the press took an interest and after an exhausting schedule of interviews, she nudged it into the Top 60. Energetic appearances on *The Tube* and *Top Of The Pops* with her raunchy, tongue-in-cheek dance routines, pushed it all the way up to number six. Madonna wondered what on earth the British thought of her. "People seeing me for the first time must have thought I was a fruitcake, a real live wire, but I can't come on and be sexy without humour."

The unshockable British record-buying public were intrigued by Madonna's brazen street-wise image, belly button and all – the midriff tops, net skirts, thick socks, crucifix earrings and copious rubber bracelets. Her vibrant act had a refreshing, rôle-reversing twist – here was a girl who had the cheek to challenge the traditionally male rock territory of the pelvis shaking, rock shockers.

But Madonna felt ill at ease, and a little unwelcome in England. Her bold and aggressive New Yorker mentality was at distinct odds with the English stiff-upper-lip. "I like England but it isn't what I'm used to. In New York people are loud and say what they think; in London you're so reserved. When I laugh out loud in the streets here, everyone stares and I feel like I'm doing something wrong.

On the tube no one speaks or smiles – in New York they assault you with noise."

Madonna concluded that, despite her new-found success, "Most times people aren't very nice to me here in England." Her next big visit would make that sentiment an understatement . . .

Madonna returned to New York to launch a visual assault on the American record buying public who still thought of her as just a pretty voice on the airwaves. For her next single, 'Borderline', she made a video for MTV in which she played a familiar role; good time girl hanging out in Manhattan's Lower West Side with the spray can gang – a tough cookie with a soft, and unmistakably sensual centre. Young Americans everywhere thought the image was cool, and she found herself being hailed as pop's sexiest blonde since her idol Debbie Harry. It was even said that she could be the next Monroe, a compliment she found flattering – and amusing. "I feel slightly entertained when people say I'm a sex symbol. I don't take it seriously but I think that if you evoke sexuality through music, it's natural."

And Madonna was trying to evoke sexuality through music, though not in the way that she was soon to be accused of by a marauding press and incensed moral parents. "'Holiday' wasn't overtly sexual, but I did try to put over some innocent sensuality when I sang it. I think the sixties Motown girl groups had that same quality."

While 'Borderline' did favourably in America and 'Holiday' conquered Europe, Madonna refused to luxuriate in her new-found success. She was itching to start on some fresh material for a second album that would be "harder and aggressive with stronger songs," and the continual release of her old songs was getting in the way. She also felt that, even though she had finally managed to crawl out of the gutter, it was important to stay in touch with the street. "I had the same friends. I went to the same divey restaurants in the East Village, and I rode the subway every day because I wasn't that noticeable, although I had a lot of young girl fans who'd start squealing on the trains and asking me if I was really Madonna."

As the release of 'Lucky Star' sent her début album sales soaring, Madonna finally started work on her second golden egg, and the man chosen to produce it was New York's hottest knob twiddler, Chic guitarist Nile Rodgers, who had recently performed miracles with David Bowie and Duran Duran.

They got on, quite literally, like a house on fire. "Nile's a passionate man who lives life to the hilt – he's a genius," enthused Madonna. "I had a lot more confidence in myself and a lot more to do with the way the album came out soundwise. I worked side by side with Nile and he was very open with me."

Madonna felt free to speak up for herself and that's just what she did. "She was more temperamental than anyone else I'd ever worked with," remembers Rodgers, "but with her it's not a bad thing. When she throws a tantrum it's because something's really bothering her. She's just fantastic."

While boyfriend Jellybean didn't figure very prominently on the new album, "He's got his own work and he's a technician rather than a musician," explained Madonna – an old acquaintance reappeared to co-write four new songs – Steve Bray. He had found it in his heart to forgive, forget and bury his pride over their professional squabble. "The relationship was too old to have something like that stand in its way," he said later.

One day in the recording studio, Madonna got a surprise visit from one of her childhood heroines, legendary soul queen Diana Ross. "She'd been recording downstairs and she and Nile are real good friends. Her kids really liked my stuff so she brought a bottle of champagne and toasted my success. I was so flattered. You hear so much about celebrities being horrible and then you meet them and they're not that way at all."

If Diana Ross was living proof that not all superstars act abominably, then so was Barbra Streisand. "When I met Barbra Streisand, she was the same – enthusiastic and encouraging."

As 'Lucky Star' and then 'Borderline' charted in England, Madonna paid a summer visit to Italy to make a big budget video for 'Like A Virgin', the title track and lead-off single from the new album. Venice was chosen as the romantic, mysterious back-

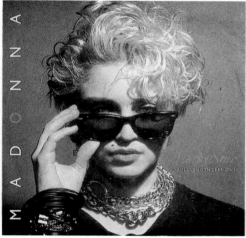

drop for her cavortings, and an element of surrealism was added in the form of one majestic extra, a real live, so-called tame lion. Madonna remembers the occasion as one of the most dangerous experiences of her short life ... "That lion didn't do anything he was supposed to do, and I ended up leaning against this pillar with his head in my crotch ... I thought he was going to take a bite out of me, so I lifted the veil I was wearing and had a stare-down with the lion and he opened his mouth and let out this huge roar. I got so frightened my heart fell in my shoe. When he finally walked away the director yelled, 'CUT' and I had to take a long breather. But I could really relate to the lion. I feel like in a past life I was a lion or a cat or something." It wasn't the last time that Madonna would have to star alongside a wild, big cat ...

Madonna returned to the comparative safety of New York to find that her 'Lucky Star' single and début album were still doing so well, that the release of 'Like A Virgin' had to be postponed; a ludicrous but lucrative state of affairs.

Nevertheless she was asked for a pre-release performance of the new song, live at the MTV video awards ceremony at Radio City. It went down well and as she left the theatre, a whole crowd of young fans turned

up to cheer her as she slipped into an awaiting limousine outside. With Madonna that night was her designer friend, Maripol, who remembers her almost bewildered response. "She was looking at all the kids and she was wondering what she was doing sitting there in the limo. She wanted to be there, with them, in the street, yelling at herself. I looked at her face and it was pure innocence and pure joy . . ."

Madonna's world was beginning to change dramatically and, inevitably, her tastes and values were going through a shake-up too. As ever, she shunned materialism; shopping spree orgies and show-off status symbols weren't what this was all about. Instead Madonna prized hard work and good health above everything. She had finally grown tired of the New York club scene, preferring to "keep a low profile and see the sun shine, take care of myself and get enough sleep because I had to look healthy on camera."

While Jellybean still revelled in the pounding, noisy night life at the Funhouse, Madonna's visits there became less and less frequent. "She became obsessed with keeping her body in shape," remembers Jellybean. "But people didn't realise how incredibly intelligent she was. She loved reading English literature; Shakespeare and Keats, she'd spend hours ploughing through their works."

F ilm director Susan Seidelman recognised the wit and wisdom of Madonna, and approached her to play the role of Susan in a low-budget showcase movie she was making called *Desperately Seeking Susan*.

Seidelman remembers their first meeting. "She was nervous and vulnerable and not at all arrogant. Sweet, but intelligent and verbal, with a sense of humour. I just started seeing her as Susan."

Madonna started to see it herself when her agent first showed her the script. The Susan character was uncannily close to Madonna's "wild, free-spirited and adventurous" nature, and the Susan lifestyle mirrored Madonna's early days as a waif on the streets of New York "living off the kindness of strangers." It could have been written specially for her – and around her.

Madonna auditioned alongside 200 actresses and it was her natural 'screen presence' that won her the part. "She has the kind of face you want to look at blown up 50 feet," enthused Seidelman. "She isn't conventionally beautiful but then neither were Bette Davis or Marlene Dietrich. I didn't choose her because she was a rock star, I'm interested in interesting people."

W hen she signed to do the movie, Madonna was an up and coming personality. When the cameras started rolling in November 1984, she was a nationwide pop star. When the filming was over at the end of the year, the 'Like A Virgin' album exploded on release and Madonna become a mega-star. This caused problems with her co-star in *Desperately Seeking Susan*, Rosanna Arquette, because Madonna was stealing all the glory. "I thought I was going to be making this small, charming film – not some rock video," she snorted to the press. Like Madonna, Arquette had left home at 17 to seek her fortune and hitchhiked cross country to Hollywood. She had paid her dues as an actress – so why should she play second fiddle to a singer?

The dynamic and fiery duo –
Rosanna Arquette and Madonna in
Desperately Seeking Susan

Madonna and Arquette had a strained and rather unusual relationship on the set. Seidelman likened them to "the two most popular cheerleaders in school – on the surface they were really friendly but underneath they couldn't wait to poke fun at each other."

Seidelman had problems with Arquette too, there were artistic conflicts that led to them both bursting into tears. When the atmosphere became too much to bear, Madonna looked to actor Mark Blum (who played Arquette's husband) for consolation. "He'd tell me a joke and chill me out."

Matters were made even worse, for Arquette that is, when Seidelman decided to use one of Madonna's new songs in the movie, a track that had only been recorded in demo form, called 'Into The Groove'. Madonna played it when some music was needed during rehearsals, and Seidelman saw its commercial potential. It was a great compliment to Madonna that the original demo was used for the soundtrack. But it was also "a drag because I was trying to establish myself as an actress, not as a singer making movies."

Madonna was also a little disappointed to find that making movies wasn't the glamorous process that Little Nonni had always imagined it to be. "It was a real drag! There was so much sitting around, it drove me crazy . . . but it's what I'd always wanted to do." And when Madonna was called on set to perform, stage-fright got the better of her. She found her first proper acting rôle almost as terrifying as her death-defying stunt with the Venetian lion. "I had a few scenes where I was really shitting bricks! A few times I was so nervous I opened my mouth and nothing came out. I think I surprised everybody though by being one of the calmest people on the set because I was in total wonderment, just soaking everything up."

Throughout the film, Madonna's rôle demanded that she indulge Susan's disgusting habit of consuming vast amounts of fattening cheese puffs. To keep her weight down, Madonna started spitting out the puffs at the end of every scene, and rising at 4.30 each morning to work out at a health club before arriving on set at 6.00. Such dedication to fitness astonished Seidelman, since filming never finished much before midnight, but Madonna's hyperactive metabolism had always caused her to suffer from insomnia, and to this

Madonna and Rosanna at the Los Angeles Pro Peace benefit.

day, she still gets by on a few hours sleep each night.

At the end of the nine weeks' filming, Madonna felt satisfied with the way the film had turned out. She believed in, and enthused about the "screwball mystery movie" she had made about "mistaken identities, stolen earrings and Egyptian symbolism . . . it was like a return to the simple caper comedies Claudette Colbert and Carole Lombard made in the thirties. They give you a taste of real life, some poignance, and leave you feeling up at the end." And Arquette had to concede that Madonna's performance was "really rather good."

Returning to the world of music, Madonna's new album entered the American chart at number 70 and it rocketed up to the number one spot in the New Year, along with the single. But there was controversy brewing over the conflicting imagery of Madonna's virginity theme, and her presentation of a sexy, voluptuous, blushing bride on the cover of the album. Without really knowing anything about the intricacies of her life story, or really giving a damn, the press started questioning her motives and her morals. How dare she call herself Madonna and sing about virginity with a BOY TOY belt slung under her navel, a rosary wrapped around her neck and a crucifix hanging from each earlobe? Surely this was a contrived attempt at blatant sacrilege?

The general consensus of critical opinion was that Madonna was a flesh peddling, ruthless sex kitten who had slept her way to success. "Despite her little girl voice, there's an undercurrent of ambition that makes her more than the latest Betty Boop," declared a *Rolling Stone* journalist, who went on to accuse her of playing the rôle of "a conniving cookie, flirting her way to the top."

Madonna landed in even deeper water by declaring on American television that her ultimate goal was to "rule the world." People couldn't see where her sense of humour was coming from at all, and Madonna had some explaining to do . . .

"I was surprised with how people reacted to 'Like A Virgin' because when I did the song, to me, I was singing about how something made me feel a certain way – brand new and fresh – and everyone else interpreted it as 'I don't want to be a virgin any more. Fuck my brains out.' That's not what I sang at all . . .

"With the crucifixes I was exorcising the extremes that my upbringing dwelt on. Putting them up on the wall and throwing darts at them. And the BOY TOY thing was a joke; a tag name given to me when I first arrived in New York because I flirted with the boys. All the graffiti artists wore their nicknames on their belt buckles." And there were times, Madonna confessed, that she liked to cast herself "in the submissive role," it was part of her heritage. "Italian men like to dominate. It's something I have felt at times in my life."

Rosenblatt at Sire Records was bewildered by the accusations and summed up the ridiculousness of the situation rather neatly when he said, "I don't understand why people find a girl looking like a girl to be at all offensive." While the press found it easier to accept Boy George's camp interpretation of femininity, Madonna's young fans ignored everything that was being said about her and rushed out to buy their copies of 'Like A Virgin' in droves. At one point it was shifting up to 75,000 copies a day – and that was in America alone.

It was getting harder and harder for Madonna to cling to normality. "And I knew it was gonna get weirder . . . I felt life was simpler when I had no money, when I barely survived. I used to worry about what I was going to eat; now I had to worry about being ripped off; if my lawyer was making the right deals; if my accountant was paying me. Boring stuff like that."

And while mutual ambition had

brought Madonna and Jellybean together, their mutual success now drove them apart. Madonna described the relationship as "Very tiring. When you're working and your private relationship is falling apart, it's hard to carry on. When you're getting on, you can't stop talking about the record business and then you wonder if you have anything else in common."

When asked about her views on marriage, the Madonna philosophy was pessimistic: "I considered it once," she said at the time. "But it seems like a silly idea now – for me. I can't conceive of living happily ever after with one person. I change so much and so my needs change also."

Somehow, success wasn't all it had been cracked up to be in Little Nonni's mind. And the going was going to get rougher . . .

Madonna's 'Material Girl' video tribute to Monroe's *Gentlemen Prefer Blondes* movie.

"I think if someone becomes hugely successful the public becomes disgusted with them and begins to wish the star would slip on a banana peel. That's a basic aspect of human nature." **Madonna.**

"Madonna will always have her detractors, but somehow little girls across the world seem to recognise a genuine hero when they see one." **Mikal Gilmore,** *Rolling Stone.*

During 1985 Madonna realised more achievements – and suffered more setbacks – than most people experience in a lifetime. She found herself growing and shrinking in public opinion with the same alarming regularity as Lewis Carroll's *Alice in Wonderland.*

In January, Madonna's 'Like A Virgin' single made number one in the United States and number two in the UK. In February, the film *Visionquest* opened in America to so-so reviews. Only two of Madonna's songs were used after all, and her 'cameo' appearance as a nightclub singer was just that. But thankfully, Madonna's songs proved more popular than the movie and 'Crazy For You' and 'The Gambler' did top ten business in the States. They did top five business in England during the course of the year – where the film was released on video and retitled *Crazy For You.*

In March, *Desperately Seeking Susan* opened in New York and 900 cinemas stateswide. The reviews were excellent, 'Into The Groove' was a hit, and the film raked in 40 million dollars.

For the moment, acting seemed to be taking over from Madonna's musical career. "I think in the back of my mind, no matter what I was learning to do, I'd always had the deepest desire to act . . . and I think, ultimately, it will outlive all my other careers," she said.

The Jellybean relationship, which Madonna admitted had been "tough going all the way," finally died a death as he became a recording star in his own right. "I think we were in 'like' rather than in 'love'," says Jellybean. "It was a good, fun time, guaranteed a laugh a day – Madonna has a great sense of humour. She's now what I consider an icon of the eighties and, yes, we're still good friends."

As Madonna made her first cool million, 'Material Girl' was the half-appropriate, half-paradoxical title of her next single. Dollars and diamonds had

never been this girl's best friend, but Marilyn Monroe had always been her favourite idol, and Madonna wanted her new video to be a tribute to the famous material girl scene in the film *Gentlemen Prefer Blondes*. Even Madonna's dress was more sophisticated than anything she had ever worn before: "I love dresses like Monroe wore, those fifties styles that were really tailored to fit a voluptuous body."

If Monroe had still been alive, she and Madonna might have had some intriguing conversations about the backlash they both suffered for portraying themselves as one hundred per cent women who generally had more fun as a result. Monroe would have argued against her image as the proverbial dumb blonde, and Madonna would have protested against the peroxide piranha tag that her critics were always trying to stick on her.

Even in this early stage of her career, Madonna could sympathise with the agonies that Monroe must have gone through. "In her time you really were a slave to the whole Hollywood machinery, and unless you had the strength to pull yourself out of it, you were trapped. I think she really didn't know what she was getting herself into and simply made herself vulnerable, and I feel a bond with that . . . I have as many vulnerabilities as I have strengths, but the strengths usually overpower the weaknesses . . . Marilyn Monroe was a victim, and I'm not."

With her 'Material Girl' concept, Madonna now found herself constantly compared to Monroe. The notorious American scandal rag, the

National Enquirer, ran a story which said she believed she was the reincarnation of Marilyn — a miraculous claim indeed when you consider that Monroe didn't die until Madonna was three years old. It was the best lie Madonna had ever read about herself.

"I had always been flattered that people compared me with Monroe because she had such a vulnerable beauty, and in videos and performance I try to give that off occasionally. But then it started to annoy me because nobody wants to be continually compared to someone else — you want people to see that you have a statement of your own to make. Ultimately I don't really identify with any one person because I don't think anyone has done what I'm doing." But one thing Madonna really did long to have in common with Monroe was her ability to "arouse so many different feelings in people." And she was certainly doing that.

While Madonna was making the video for 'Material Girl', an admirer paid a visit to the set and introduced himself. Exit DJ Jellybean and enter actor Sean Penn. The hot blooded, Hollywood Brat Packer with a reputation for letting his fists do

the talking when aroused. "He had a rebellious bad boy image — the same as I did, only for a girl," said Madonna.

She was magnetised by Penn's fiery charms. She had always liked "dark brooding men with rough tempers." She also joked that she had always loved "small furry animals with big eyes that stay up all night and hang off the trees by their tails. Maybe that's what attracted me to Sean!"

Sean wooed Madonna by taking her to see Monroe's grave in California on an early date, and a whirlwind romance followed. The couple felt bonded by a kindred, emotional intensity. They discovered their birthdays were only one day apart. But the heavens that joined them together, soon put them prematurely asunder, as Sean had to leave for Atlanta to start work on his new film, *At Close Range*, and Madonna embarked upon her first tour of America. The courtship would continue over the telephone, but at least that way the press were slow to catch on that they were crazy about each other.

In April Madonna opened her 38-date nationwide Virgin tour in Seattle, Washington, at the Paramount Theatre. The tour would take in 28 cities and play to 300,000 fans. All the tickets for all the concerts

Sean Penn shuns the press, as always, as he and Madonna leave New York's NBC studios after appearing on *Saturday Night Live*.

had sold out within two hours, and a new record had been set in New York, where the 17,622 tickets for her three Radio City shows sold out in 34 minutes exactly. Madonna had never been more popular; she had six consecutive US Top Ten singles, all in the Top 40 simultaneously, making her the most successful female solo artist – ever.

The hundreds of thousands of young fans who turned up to her concerts were mainly girls who had ransacked their mothers' make-up bags and wardrobes to copy Madonna's lacy look. They had studied her image in *Desperately Seeking Susan* and gone to great pains to get every detail right; ratting their hair, exposing their navels, and wearing the all-essential BOY TOY belts, fingerless gloves, and Catholic 'jewellery' which the big stores, keen to cash in on the whole phenomenon, stocked a-plenty.

French designer Maripol had designed Madonna's stage wear, and her Maripolitan shop on Bleecker Street had never done such good business. One New York department store devoted an entire 'Madonnaland' floor to selling 'the look', and the formerly frumpy lingerie industry clapped their hands in glee as youngsters started buying pretty bras again. Even the Paris fashion houses sent their models swaggering down the catwalk in Madonna-based designs. Meanwhile, the official tour merchandisers announced record profits just halfway through the schedule, as Madonna t-shirts disappeared at the rate of one every six seconds.

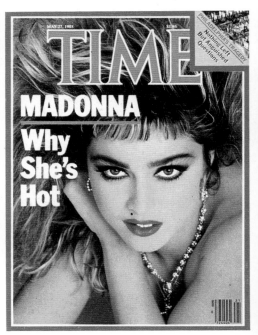

Madonna makes the cover of America's big selling news weekly *Time* on May 27, 1985.

It was the invasion of the 'wannabes', as Madonna's followers came to be known, and Madonna was initially bewildered by their devotional fanaticism. "There were all these girls idolising me and dressing like me and I couldn't understand why it was happening. It was a mystery to me why they were copying my hodge-podge, tongue-in-cheek tart outfits. But it finally came to make sense – for so long young women have been told that there are certain ways they mustn't look if they want to get ahead in life, and there I was, dressing in a forbidden way and obviously in charge of my life and my career. I was saying, 'I can look sexy if I choose to and still be smart'."

Just as Madonna liberated herself in her teens by putting on the pointy bras and tight sweaters that her heroines wore, so America's adolescent youth looked to Madonna as a rôle model for the eighties. It had been an age since a female singer had come along and created an accessible image that aspiring young rebels could adopt. You didn't have to look like a freak, or have good cheekbones and a perfect body to join the Madonna cult. Any ordinary girl with a sense of humour could cut it as a 'wannabe'.

"I certainly wasn't born with a perfect body," laughed Madonna. "I'm 5' 4" and I feel like a shrimp – I probably look taller 'cos I've got such a big mouth. And I always wanted to be flat-chested so I didn't have to wear a bra."

As for John F. Kennedy Junior, Boy George had introduced Madonna to him when they both attended his New York birthday party. The press saw a good hook and accused her of flirting with the late President's playboy son – and the ghost of Monroe. Boy George made one of his typically bitchy comments, scoffing: "Comparing Marilyn Monroe with Madonna is like comparing Raquel Welch with the back of a bus." At least he had a sense of humour.

But it wasn't just the image they admired, it was Madonna's attitude, the way she believed in herself and could help her disciples do the same. "I have a positive attitude about life and I think my fans see that. There are so many negative things happening around the world: incurable diseases, famine, the threat of nuclear war. What kind of thing is it for children to grow up with that fear? I think it's really important for them to have something to inspire them and take them out of that – not so they don't even think about it –

but to realise that there are also some positive things going on."

Madonna's concerts were intended to be a celebration of physical awareness, joy, humour, honesty and the good things in life, sometimes even the simple things. "The things that inspire me to make music are the things that arouse my curiosity and make me happy in life . . . every day I try to write in a journal, jotting down thoughts or maybe something I read that impressed me . . . everything inspires me: a great book or a movie, an expression in someone's eye, children or old men walking down the street. You know what I like to do when I go to parties? I like talking to the butlers and the janitors and stuff – they're the funniest

– they inspire me."

That first night in Seattle, the 'wannabes' screamed impatiently for their idol as Madonna took up her position backstage behind a big screen. Full of "nerves and excitement" as the screen began to rise, she prepared herself mentally: "This is me. And here I am for all you people . . ."

Making her way down the long white staircase wearing a psychedelic jacket, her heart on her sleeve, she was ready to teach the eager 'wannabes' how to lose their inhibitions, kick ass and raunch it up. "You people are too shy," she shouted to her

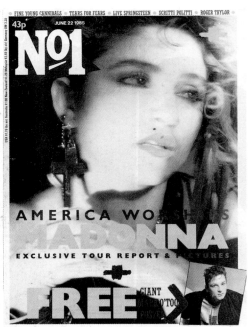

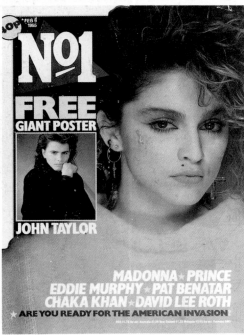

Madonnamania: Britain's *No.1* pop magazine puts Madonna on their February and June 1985 covers.

audience, "You don't have to be shy with me . . ." When Madonna saw the expressions in their eyes she felt an "ecstasy and thrill" that fired her saucy performance. Standing astride a fluorescent ghettoblaster and rocking back and forth she said suggestively: "Every lady has a box, mine is different because it makes music. You're gonna have to help me make my box talk."

For 'Like A Virgin', Madonna swept onto the stage in a white silk wedding dress with a 20-foot train and crawled between her guitarist's legs, knowing full well that the press were going to have a field day with her titillating antics. "Do you believe in me?" she implored her fans. Of course they did. "What else do you believe in? Good things, right? Do you believe that dreams come true?" They believed they had come true for Madonna, and that meant there was hope for them all.

With each song, Madonna aimed to reach out and establish an intimate rapport with her fans, determined to live up to their vision of her as a fearless super-heroine – a custodian of the great American dream. She was a high wire flier without a safety net, and though she felt like "a warrior" when she went onstage, she wanted them to see that she was vulnerable inside – as vulnerable as the fans at the front of the stage who were crushing each other to get nearer.

"When you're singing a song you are making yourself very vulnerable. It's almost like crying in front of people . . ."

When Madonna sang 'Material Girl' she deliberately mocked the image that the public had of her. "Throughout the song I went up to the guys in the band and they gave me pearls and diamonds and money and I stuffed it down my shirt and went crazy with it. At the end I said to the audience, 'Do you think I'm a material girl?' and they all went, 'Yeah'. Then I said, 'I'm not' and took it all off and threw it into the audience. If you can't make jokes about yourself then you're not going to be happy. You'll be the saddest person that ever lived . . . in my concerts there are so many moments when I just stand there and laugh at myself."

F or her grand finale, Madonna conjured the memory of Little Nonni as a strict, fatherly voice came across the speakers scolding; "MADONNA, YOU'RE COMING HOME RIGHT NOW, YOUNG LADY." Madonna played the frustrated little girl as she back-

answered, "Oh Daddy, do I hafta?"

As the tour made its way to her home town of Detroit, it was Madonna's real father who joined her on stage for that endearing moment. Sylvio agreed to brave the multitudes and Madonna primed him for his supporting rôle. "I said, 'Dad, when you come onstage, think back to those days when you were really mad at me, like that talent show I did in my bathing suit with the strobe light.' I said, 'Think of that, and how you wanted to yank me off the stage.' And he did! Boy, he just about dismembered me. When I came offstage I was so hysterical I just collapsed laughing. That was a total release, because I felt my father was finally seeing what I do for a living." It was only a pity that Madonna's real mother wasn't there to see it too.

In June the Virgin tour climaxed in New York at Madison Square Garden. "There's a place across the street," Madonna told the crowd, "where I used to look out the window at the Garden and say, 'I wonder if I'll ever get in there . . .'" The days of smelly rooming houses and garbage can meals were well and truly behind her and she was going to fight to keep it that way.

But there was a whole stack of people out there who couldn't wait to start dishing some dirt. Her ex-manager Camille Barbone sued Madonna for 'premature dismissal', and received a small settlement. As she stewed angrily in her own bitter juices, it occurred to her that someone might actually pay good money for her side of the Madonna story. At the same time, a whole bunch of unscrupulous nude photographers realised that, if people were so keen to see Madonna in the flesh, then they could certainly oblige. It was merely a question of finding the highest bidder.

W hile Sean Penn was still filming in Atlanta, Madonna was connected with a whole string of men-she-was-supposed-to-be-dating, specifically Prince, Billy Idol, Don Johnson, David Lee Roth, and even John F. Kennedy Junior. The truth of the matter was that Madonna had met Prince when she was on tour in San Francisco and discovered that, like her, he was "competitive and had something to prove"; she had once considered doing a song with Billy Idol because they were both "white and plastic and blonde"; Don Johnson had taken it upon himself to try and entice her with flowers, and kept pestering her to make a record with him; and she had

once invited David Lee Roth to a party.

The summer of 1985 would prove to be eventful to say the least. Chartwise, Madonna's single 'Into The Groove' had entered the British charts at number four – the highest début position ever for a record by a woman. On the strength of this success, Warners re-released her first album, and the 'Like A Virgin' album with 'Into The Groove' and 'Holiday' added to the track listing. Meanwhile, Madonna's passionate romance with Sean Penn continued and they tried to spend some quiet time together in a Tennessee Inn. One Sunday morning Madonna awoke to hear the sound of mystical wedding bells – ringing in her head. "I was jumping up

and down on the bed, performing one of my morning rituals and all of a sudden Sean got this look in his eye. I felt like I knew what he was thinking and said, 'Whatever you're thinking, I'll say yes to.' That was his chance, so he proposed."

But something had to mar the excitement. Two freelance newshounds started snooping around the couple, and as a ham-fisted protest for peace and privacy, Sean lashed out in his own inimitable style, attacking them with a rock. Madonna stood helplessly by and Sean left Tennessee with a suspended sentence hanging over his head. Somehow, Madonna was going to have to learn to cope with her husband-to-be's violent outbursts.

News of the imminent wedding was leaked immediately in the *New York Daily News*. The big day was apparently set for August, when Sean was scheduled to finish filming *At Close Range*. The paper also predicted that the pair couldn't wait to make a film together. Of course, it was obvious to all the media folks, that Madonna was clearly marrying this (relatively unknown) actor to further her movie career, even if she had managed to do pretty well on her own up until now.

Madonna's view of marriage was

rosy, and she was already planning ahead. "I think getting married is probably very challenging, and I would definitely like to have a child. I've heard wonderful things about childbirth from people my age. I'm saying it like it's baking a cake or something, but I know there will be more to it than that."

Bob Guccione, the publisher of soft porn magazine *Penthouse*, was pretty excited too. "A great number of Madonna nudes had all surfaced at once and we had first choice," he said. "They came from many different sources – photography teachers and their students, amateurs and professionals."

Playboy, Guccione's main rival, got their share of nudes too, and the fight was on to see who could hit the stands first. And what better timing than to rush release them just before Madonna was due to play before the whole world on Live Aid?

Guccione rubbed salt into Madonna's wounds by having the nerve to offer her a million dollars to pose for a new, exclusive Penthouse session. Not surprisingly her agent's only comment on the whole sorry affair was "Madonna has absolutely nothing to say." But *Penthouse* went one sordid step further. "They did something really nasty," remembers Madonna. "They sent copies of the magazine to Sean."

On July 10, Hugh Hefner's *Playboy* beat *Penthouse* to the stands and by July 11, the pictures had winged their way across the Atlantic to appear in Britain's cheapest tabloids with the usual, unimaginative flurry of headlines: MAD FOR MADONNA, NAUGHTY NAUGHTY MADONNA, and NAUGHTY (BUT VERY NICE) MADONNA. Though the pictures weren't promoted in a flattering light, they were actually quite innocent and tame, nothing to be particularly ashamed of.

"When people saw them they thought, 'What's the big deal here?'" remembers Madonna. "But I can't say I wasn't devastated by the experience. Sean kept saying, 'Look, this is all going to blow over.' But nobody wants their skeletons to come out of the closet. No matter how successful you want to be, you can never ever anticipate that kind of attention – the grand scale of it all.

"The thing that annoyed me most was the fact that, for the first time in several years of careful planning and knowing what was going to happen, I felt really out of control. It took me by surprise . . . it reminded me of the time when I was a little girl at school and the nuns used to come along and lift your dress up in front of everybody to check what colour knickers you were wearing. It's embarrassing because you're just not ready for it and you feel so exposed.

"Now I look back and I feel silly that I ever got so upset, but I remember feeling that same, end-of-the-world feeling the day my step-mother told me I couldn't wear stockings to school. I cried for hours and thought I wouldn't live through the next day. You think it's the end of the world, and then one day it's not."

A busy schedule of rehearsals for Live Aid helped keep Madonna from dwelling too much on the whole fiasco. Her musical director, Pat Leonard, who was with her during that dreadful week commends her to this day for her incredible ability to stay so cool. "She only said one thing in reference to those photos. I was making fun of her about something and she said, 'Aw, Lenny, get off my back. I've had a rough week.' That's all she said."

Madonna kicks ass at Live Aid despite the embarrassment of the porn pin-ups.

It wasn't easy for Madonna to make her first public appearance since the nude episode at Live Aid, before 90,000 people in Philadelphia's JFK Stadium, and an estimated globewide audience of two billion. But the show had to go on. "Part of me felt about 'this' big and another part of me was saying, 'I'll be damned if I'm gonna let that make me feel down. I'm gonna get out there and kick ass, get this dark cloud out from over my head.'"

It didn't help that Bette Midler introduced Madonna onstage with a sarcastic speech that kicked her when she was down, calling her "A woman who pulled herself up by her bra straps and has been known to let them down occasionally." But Madonna broached the subject with her usual defiant aplomb by announcing "I ain't taking shit off today!"

Madonna had the last laugh. Backstage, Sean was with her, holding her hand all the way, and she finally met up with one of her favourite musical idols. The Pretenders were sharing the same set of trailers and Chrissie Hynde came over for a chat. They were to meet again in similar, Madonna-bashing circumstances, and forge a close and genuine friendship. Madonna's brave performance at Live Aid endeared her even

further to her fans, and the sales of her entire back catalogue went sky-rocketing. It hadn't been such a bad day after all. "It was a great day and I'd happily do it again," she said later.

But there were still a few influential narrow-minded people who would only associate the name of Madonna with so much dirty laundry. The Mayor of her hometown, Bay City in Michigan, revoked his decision to honour the local star with the Key to the City. "It would not be in good taste to give it to her now," he said. And when Madonna made a bid to buy a plush apartment in the exclusive New York San Remo Building, a place where select media bods were only admitted by a show of hands, she was voted unclean by the residents committee. A New Yorker's home is his castle . . . "If we let her in," said an anonymous board member, "we'll have to let everybody in." Only actress Diane Keaton supported her.

And there were several self-righteous organisations who condemned Madonna for encouraging young girls to follow in her 'degrading' footsteps, namely Jerry Falwell's Moral Majority and the Parents' Music Resource Centre. Hellbent on trying to get her records banned, none of them stopped to think that, in their young days, most of them

Madonna joins The Thompson Twins at Live Aid.

had doubtless lapped up the forbidden pleasures of Elvis Presley's X-rated pelvis.

"Basically, a bunch of moralists had gotten together and decided that the majority of the lyrics and images that a lot of pop artists were projecting was injurious to the minds of their children," said Madonna. "Most of the words in my songs have double entendres or lots of different meanings, but I'm not using any offensive words or profanity at all. I think all of my songs have an element of desire or flirtation but it's never, 'Come on baby, let's get in the bed and get down to it.' It's not like that.

"I think ultimately children, more than anybody, sense the realness of somebody. I don't think they attach themselves to a person and look up to them unless there's some innate goodness or sweetness to them. You let go of that trust and innocence, and that intuitive psychic ability to see that in people as you grow older."

And it wasn't just the moralists who condemned Madonna. Feminists were at it too, adhering to their topsy turvy belief that the only way to compete in a so-called man's world was to try and act like one, even dress like one. But Madonna had actually created a new kind of feminism; why deny your own true nature when you can be smart and feminine at the same time? And, yes, sexy too. Was that such a crime?

"They said that I'd set women back 30 years. Well, in the fifties women weren't ashamed of their bodies," counters Madonna. "They luxuriated in their sexuality and they were very strong in their femininity. Women aren't like men ... I've only recently come to understand that to some women I represent a kind of liberation for females. I give young

women strength and hope. So in that respect I feel my behaviour, my art, is feminist."

In August Madonna made record breaking history in the UK: 'Into The Groove' became her first English number one, and the summer re-release of 'Holiday' peaked at number two,

becoming the first single by a woman to reach the Top 10 on two separate occasions. She also joined The Beatles and John Lennon in managing to hold the top two positions in the chart at the same time. In fact she had three singles in the UK Top 20 during August, and the only other woman to have ever placed more than two simultaneously was Irish songstress Ruby Murray way back in 1955.

August 16 was Madonna's 26th birthday and, after a short, sweet and action-packed six-month courtship, also her wedding day. She and Sean had planned a lavish but hopefully quiet wedding in a secret location, a beach house, with a clifftop view in Malibu, Los Angeles. But somehow the press knew just where to find them and the clifftop ceremony made them vulnerable to snoopers. As the nuptials began, to Madonna's horror, a host of newsmongering helicopters whirled defiantly towards them and merged in a deafening, low flying formation for an unofficial photo-call.

"It was almost too much," remembers Madonna. "I mean, I didn't think I was going to be getting married with 13 helicopters flying over my head. It turned into a circus. In the end, I was laughing. You couldn't have written it in a movie. No one would have believed it. It was like a Busby Berkeley musical."

Madonna and Sean added a touch of slapstick humour to make the wedding really swing. They cut their cake and threw handfuls of icing and cream into each other's faces as the reception dinner and dance grooved along to the sounds of the forties and fifties. "We'd chosen music by Cole Porter, Bing Crosby, Ella Fitzgerald, and Sarah Vaughan – the roots of rock 'n' roll." Phase two of the party began at midnight – on Sean Penn's birthday.

Next day, the *News Of The World* ran some extremely blurred pictures and the headline, MADONNA'S GROOM IN TIPSY PARTY BRAWL. HE THROWS BLOWS AT PHOTOGRAPHER. Apparently, a British lensman gatecrashed the wedding and Sean allegedly attacked him while Madonna screamed for help. How unreasonable of him.

The newly weds spent a peaceful honeymoon on the Caribbean paradise island of Antigua where, mercifully, the locals respected their privacy and left them alone. It was the lull before the storm.

Madonna was rumoured to be worth eight million dollars now, and it was time for a few more greedy skeletons to jump out of the cupboard and cash in on her success. Jon Lewicki threatened to release *A Certain Sacrifice* on video. Madonna took the matter to court, protesting that the second rate film traded on her name and her image unfairly, but the case was thrown out, and Lewicki made hundreds of

thousands. In September, ex-manager Camille Barbone finally exorcised her longstanding grudge by selling a two-part exclusive scoop to the *News Of The World*. BOY TOY MADONNA LEFT A TRAIL OF BROKEN HEARTS and I CREATED A MONSTER WHO TURNED ON ME were the sensational headlines. Camille talked dirty: "Madonna loves sex and would go after any man she wanted. She seduced men the way men seduce women … Madonna had more than 100 lovers but she didn't keep score." During Camille's year-long association with the star, that meant Madonna was seducing an average of two

lovers per day, in between working and gigging with Bray at Gotham studios. It didn't sound very plausible – but it did sound like sour grapes.

September also saw the English editions of the *Playboy* and *Penthouse* nudes. *Playboy*'s presentation wasn't too tasteless but as for Penthouse: "Madonna knows that forbidden fruit is the greatest temptation and that nothing incites the lust of a crowd like the illusion of virginity poised for the taking … central to the Madonna mystique is her notoriety as a sexual shark." *Penthouse* made no bones about their view of Madonna, they accused her of "effing her way to the top."

The *News Of The World*'s coverage of Madonna's 'punch-up' wedding.

paparazzi trailed her everywhere, springing out from street corners when she went shopping, jumping from bushes when she went jogging in Central Park. "I had a heart attack every time it happened. I had to deal with that constant fear. The way they took those pictures – it was like they were raping me. It took me at least an hour to come down from that shock every time it happened."

Madonna cast a philosophical inner-eye over her situation. "There's always going to be the adversary, the antagonist, the good and the bad, the yin and the yang. Maybe the negative exists so we can see the positive."

Madonna began to dread interviews and photo sessions altogether. "Sometimes I'll be doing a photo session with someone that I've done a lot of work with before and, all of a sudden, I feel like they've seen too much and I don't want them to look at me any more. Usually I'm pretty outgoing and gregarious but I can be really shy about things too."

If there was one calming influence in her life, it was Sean. "Now that I'm in love, all the songs I write, I feel like I do it all for him. I think, 'Would Sean like it?' Love inspires me and Sean inspires me."

Madonna found escapism in movies, music and books – the things she had always enjoyed, but had so little time for lately. "I'm kinda having my childhood now," she said at the time, as she went to the movies "practically every day" and listened to classical music with Sean who had turned her on to Brahms. "My favourite music is baroque, Vivaldi, Bach and Handel's Water Music. I love Mozart and Chopin because there's a real sweet feminine quality about a lot of their music." And of course Madonna was still an ardent bookworm, gobbling up classics by Hemingway and Lawrence, French writers, biographies, poetry and Jack Kerouac. "I can't wait to move into my house so I can have a room full of books on the walls. Man, I love to read."

Madonna also began to meditate on the prospect of becoming a mother. "I would love to have a child. I really want to watch somebody grow and have a personal effect on their life from the very beginning." Press rumours circulated that she must be pregnant, but when Madonna appeared on an episode of the American comedy show *Saturday Night Live*, in November she quipped before a commercial break, "I'm not pregnant – and we'll be right back!"

But still Madonna's fans refused to be conned by the commotion. As *Desperately Seeking Susan* opened in the UK, she received glowing reviews and her album 'Like A Virgin' reached number one after 44 weeks in the charts. In 1985 she had sold 20 million records worldwide and had indeed risen to the lofty heights that Freddie De Mann had predicted. She was up there with Michael Jackson, though the press were convinced that Madonna would disappear just as 'quickly' as she had arrived.

Back in New York, still living in the same apartment with only a few possessions to her name, Madonna began to pay the ultimate price of fame – a complete and utter invasion of privacy. During her tour she had sampled her first real taste of Madonna mania when she tried going for a walk in New Orleans one day. "I put a hat on and pulled it down low, but I stepped onto the kerb and everybody said 'There's Madonna'. I felt caged in hotel rooms wherever I went."

Determined not to "sit around and concentrate on my fame or how popular I was," Madonna made the effort to live a relatively normal life in New York. But the

Madonna's raunchy live routine on
The Virgin Tour.

A scene from the disastrous romantic movie *Shanghai Surprise.*

"Twenty years ago there was a lot more mystery about movie stars, musicians and public figures. Nowadays they want to rape your soul . . . it takes all the magic out of Hollywood and it's really upsetting to me."
Madonna

In 1986, the unlikely figure of Walt Disney – among the most conservative business empires in the US – paid a tribute to the star who has often been described as having a voice like 'Minnie Mouse on helium' by revamping Minnie in Madonna's image. Little Minnie was restyled with lacy gloves, trainers and jewellery in an effort to relaunch her career.

Meanwhile, the real Madonna had discovered a promising new film script adapted from a book called *Faraday's Flowers*. It was the story of a girl called Gloria who leaves America during the depression to seek adventure in Shanghai and become a missionary. Madonna thought the film would be a challenge for her as Gloria's character " . . . was someone very removed from how I actually am, someone who didn't know how to express her emotions . . . I still needed a rôle where I could prove to people that I could really act."

Madonna asked Sean for his opinion on the script and, as chance would have it . . . "He really liked the male rôle so we looked at each other and thought, 'Maybe this would be a good one to do together.' We were both setting ourselves up for a challenge; the challenge of being married and working together. A lot of people said it was a sure way to end a relationship and that we'd be getting

divorced afterwards." But divorce never reared its ugly head – at least not on this occasion.

The plot for the film, called *Shanghai Surprise*, with its elements of adventure and reluctant love reminded the couple of Bogart and Hepburn's charming classic *The African Queen*, and that was how they envisioned it turning out. To set the mood, Madonna finally dropped her wild child image and wore her hair long and wavy, like an old fashioned vintage movie queen.

George Harrison's Hand Made Films were behind the movie, and newcomer Jim Goddard took the director's chair. He came highly recommended to Sean by actor Martin Sheen who worked with him on an American mini-series about the life of President Kennedy. The author of the book *Faraday's Flowers*, Tony Kendrick, thought Madonna was perfect for the part. "It's a brilliant piece of casting. On the surface Madonna's character is a shy uptight missionary, but it turns out she's not as strait-laced as all that."

In January, Madonna and Sean flew to China to find Shanghai, a bizarre and alien city. "We arrived in the middle of the night but we couldn't sleep, so we ended up walking around the streets on this cold morning. It was still dark and the streets were filled with people doing their traditional, slow motion Tai Chi exercises. It was so dreamlike." The real beauty of it all was that absolutely no one knew who or what Madonna was. "I loved that and because I had blond hair they thought I was a

Madonna and Hand Made film's ex-Beatle boss George Harrison.

Martian from outer space."

But the journalists in Hong Kong – her next stop – knew her only too well – and that was when all the trouble began. Not only were there hordes of photographers and reporters from local English-speaking newspapers, but the UK press had flown out to 'greet' her as well, and the crowds started following the film crew around, demanding their god-given right for a story.

To make matters worse, Madonna began to realise that their director was in way above his head. Goddard's television experience wasn't enough to carry him through a film; he just didn't have an eye for the big screen. "It was downhill from the second day," she recalled later. *Shanghai Surprise* was mutating into an Oriental nightmare. Madonna suffered second-film-jitters as she feared her acting ability might fall short of her husband's high standards, but in working with Sean she discovered his real strength as an actor, "I had all these feelings of insecurity, I kept thinking . . . 'I'll be a terrible actress and he won't love me any more.' But Sean is a very giving actor, he never makes you feel like you're not adding up a scene. That's his main thing when he's making a movie – he makes it work for whoever's in the scene with him. Strangely enough, we never got along better."

aving regained her confidence, there was still the problem of Hong Kong itself to contend with. "We were in a very foreign country working with a Chinese crew and there were communication problems. I had to keep walking around in thin cotton blouses in very cold weather, there were big black rats underneath our trailers and people were always going down with food poisoning. I kept saying, 'I can't wait till I can look back on all this.' It was a survival test — all the odds were against us."

To create an authentic, old Shanghai atmosphere, the film crew were forced to shoot in seedy low-life slums where they found themselves intruding on genuine gangster territory. The Chinese mobs who controlled the area exploited the film crew for every Hong Kong dollar they had by obstructing their way and demanding massive payoffs.

"We were at this one location for 18 hours because they'd blocked the only exit, and this guy wanted 50 thousand dollars to

move," remembers Madonna. "That went on every day, and nobody would help us."

The filming, a never ending nightmare, continued on the nearby island of Macaou. Madonna and Sean escaped safely from the gangsters, only to find a snooping photographer lurking in their hotel room, and Sean promptly twisted his camera strap round his neck. Matters were now so bad that George Harrison had to be flown over to try and keep the peace.

"Sean and I took turns being strong

and not letting things affect us too much. There was a time when I was so overtaken by it, and I was crying, and he said, 'Don't worry baby, we'll make it work.' Then in two weeks he'd be miserable and I'd be holding him up saying, 'We'll get through this'."

I n February 21, Madonna flew to Heathrow airport on an earlier flight than Sean to begin filming indoor scenes at their UK locations: an old Sanatorium in Virginia Water, Surrey, and Shepperton Studios, Middlesex. The paparazzi were out in force to snap her airport arrival for posterity, and as Madonna's bodyguards struggled to help her into her awaiting Mercedes, the chauffeur tried to pull away with everyone crowding around. Paparazzi threw themselves on to the bonnet and the man from *The Sun* sprained his foot.

It was really no surprise that someone had got hurt – and it made an excellent front page story. The man from *The Sun* came up with an Oscar winning performance as he posed in the middle of the road, looking for all the world as if he was dying. Pictures of the wounded trooper made the front page of *The Sun* with the dramatic headline MAIMED BY MADONNA, and the press invented a new nickname for Madonna and her husband – they were referred to as The Poison Penns for the remainder of their stay.

War had been declared. It now became a matter of honour for the paparazzi to get scoop pictures of the couple; and for Sean to protect their privacy. The journalists set up camp outside the Surrey Sanitorium, where they tried to get past security by disguising themselves as cooks, electricians, and even Madonna doubles. One photographer escaped with pictures stolen from the set, and a radio reporter was dragged out of London's Park Lane Hotel when she was discovered in the ladies' toilets armed with a tape recorder.

Finally, to try and defuse the situation, George Harrison – a man not unused to hysterical scenes – again assumed the rôle of peace keeper, and proposed a press conference with Madonna on March 6 at the Kensington Roof Gardens. Uninvited guests tried to storm the venue by sneaking into service lifts, and Madonna's car was besieged on arrival. "Do you really want us to get beaten up and torn apart?" pleaded an exasperated George Harrison.

Now it was a battle of wits – the press fired taunting questions at the conference. Did Madonna and Sean fight on the set? Did Madonna really think she was up to making a proper movie yet? And did Madonna intend to apologise for her behaviour towards the Press? "I have nothing to apologise for," she replied, politely and firmly. The conference came to an ugly conclusion when George Harrison let down his hair and accused the gathering of "behaving like animals," to which a reporter added snidely, "Talking of animals – where's Sean Penn today?" Game, set and match to the press . . .

W hen Madonna left she had to have police protection to leave the building in one piece, and she awoke the next day to hear a droning tape-loop of her voice repeating, "I have nothing to apologise for . . . I have nothing to apologise for . . ." on a local radio station. Surprisingly, the

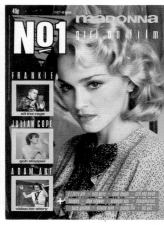

papers all but ignored the press conference, except to say that Madonna had been snooty, moody and scowling.

"I thought to myself, 'Am I really this awful? Or does Lucretia Borgia step out in my shoes when I'm not looking?'" Madonna wasn't sure if she ever wanted to set foot in England again, but decided to reserve judgement until such time as she could look back and laugh at the whole affair – at the year she had been hounded to the four corners of the earth.

George Harrison, whom Madonna described as being . . . "a sweet sort of hapless character who doesn't have a mean bone in his body," praised her for her professionalism throughout, and sympathised. "In the sixties all people could do was knock The Beatles so I've been through it all myself . . ." He also confidently predicted that "This film is going to be a box office smash . . ."

It wasn't. It was a terrible box office flop in both America and England, and Madonna's greatest mistake since the day she posed nude. "It was a truly miserable experience that I learned a lot from and don't regret.

"The film was edited as an adventure movie and they left out all the stuff that was its saving grace. They cut all my major scenes down to nothing which made me look like an airhead girl without any character."

While in London, Madonna and Sean met up again with Chrissie Hynde, whose husband Jim Kerr was on a year-long tour with Simple Minds. The two couples became firm friends and saw each other when Chrissie returned to America to do some recording in Los Angeles.

Madonna also had work to do in the recording studio when she returned home. Her third album 'True Blue' was due out in the summer – but first she went straight to a meeting to discuss another film she was hoping to make called *Blind Date*. "I was supposed to have approval of the leading man and the director, and they didn't tell me they'd already hired Bruce Willis. That . . . just didn't work out," she said mysteriously.

Madonna and Sean on stage at Aids Benefit at Madison Sq Gar

Madonna had full approval on the way her new album turned out. For the first time she helped produce and write all the songs, along with partners Pat Leonard and Steve Bray. "She was around for every note," commented Leonard. "She

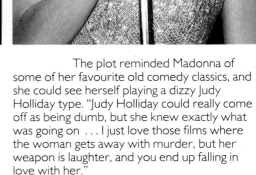

doesn't like musical rules and her instincts just turn the songs into 'Madonna' records."

"I like to have control but I'm not a tyrant," says Madonna. "I like to be surrounded by really talented, intelligent people who I trust, and ask them for their advice and get their input too."

The album, which was dedicated to Sean, " . . . the coolest guy in the universe," shot to the top of the charts across the world and the haunting lead-off ballad 'Live To Tell' also featured as the theme for Sean's movie *At Close Range.*

The second release 'Papa Don't Preach', was a song which Madonna predicted would be highly controversial. It was about a young pregnant girl who, against her parents' wishes, decides to keep her baby. This time the complainant was an organisation called Planned Parenthood who claimed she was romanticising teenage pregnancy, but the anti-abortionists were behind her. For the video, Madonna had another new haircut, this time blonde, short and gamine. Her image was becoming increasingly sophisticated; long gone

were the crucifixes and rosaries – though she was now throwing darts at the Catholic doctrines that presumed to control a woman's body. The third single, 'True Blue', was accompanied by a video in which Madonna played a stripper in a peep-hole show, and MTV declared its release date, October 14, True Blue Day.

By the end of an already exhausting year, Madonna had started work on her third film, "a physical, screwball comedy" called *Who's That Girl.* The part had been brought to her attention by director James Foley, one of the Penn's best friends, who had worked with Madonna before on video and with Sean on *At Close Range.* "He knew that I'd wanted to do a comedy for a long time so it was like my reward. There was just something about the character, the contrasts in her nature, how she was tough on one side and vulnerable on the other – that I thought I could take and make my own."

The plot reminded Madonna of some of her favourite old comedy classics, and she could see herself playing a dizzy Judy Holliday type. "Judy Holliday could really come off as being dumb, but she knew exactly what was going on . . . I just love those films where the woman gets away with murder, but her weapon is laughter, and you end up falling in love with her."

Madonna's character, Nikki Finn, was another streetwise woman with a soft heart. Wrongly convicted of murder, she sets out to prove her innocence with the aid of a lawyer, played by Griffin Dunne. And bringing back memories of that Venetian video with the lion, Madonna and Dunne had to star alongside a trained cougar.

"I had a lot in common with Nikki. She's courageous and sweet and funny and misjudged. But she clears her name in the end, and that's always good to do. I'm continuously doing that with the public . . ."

Foley was a little worried that Madonna's now awesome star status might alienate the film crew, but from day one, she

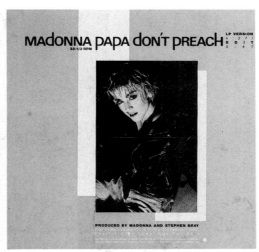

made sure that didn't happen by learning all their names and fooling around with them. The crew responded by making sure her every need was catered for. Foley remembers: "They'd run around getting her boxes to sit on, and when it got cold they'd build her a little booth with a heater and she'd sit in there like a princess and love it. She's the greatest flirt of all time." But Madonna could also be stubborn, and there was a time when Foley had to get down on his knees and kiss the girl's feet in order to get her to overdub a line that she didn't feel needed overdubbing. "She can be bossy," laughs Foley. "That's my father in me," grins Madonna.

Madonna and Sean spent some time living apart while she stayed close to the film set and Sean remained at their new, opulent Malibu beach house. A whole batch of rumours started that Madonna wanted to leave him because she could no longer stand Sean's reckless and violent tantrums, the slugging and spitting at the photographers who trailed them everywhere.

"From the time we got married, people wanted our marriage to fail," sighs Madonna. "And that did put a lot of strain on our relationship. It's been a test of love to get through it all. A lot of the times, the press would make up the most awful things that we have never done, fights that we never had. Then sometimes we would have a fight and we'd read about it, and it would be almost spooky, like they'd predicted it or bugged our phones."

While Madonna admits that in the beginning of her career she had invited controversy, press and publicity, and always been outgoing enough to handle it and strong enough to rise above it, she insists that Sean had never invited that kind of attention. "He's a very serious actor and he isn't interested in having a Hollywood star image, so it took him by surprise. We deal with it differently. I don't like violence. I never condone hitting anyone.

But on the other hand, I understood Sean's anger and, believe me, I've wanted to hit them many times, but I realise it only makes things worse ... the press went out of their way to pick on Sean, to the point where they would walk down the street and kind of poke at him and say, 'C'mon, hit me.'

"When they insult me, he wants to protect me. As inefficient as his methods might be, he has a way of thinking, an integrity, and he sticks with what he believes in, no matter what. There's not many people who do that. I'm inspired by Sean and shocked by him at the same time."

In November 1986, a British DJ was given permission to fly to America for an exclusive interview for Radio One, in which Madonna set the record straight revealing that, despite some tension, she had no plans for divorce. "When we're apart we write lots of letters and run up huge bills on the phone. To me our love feels like a huge hand that comes around my whole body. Sometimes it's all furry and warm and sometimes it's all scratchy and it hurts." Meanwhile Sean made a TV appearance on the *Tonight Show* and admitted to Johnny Carson that his violent behaviour was a sign of 'immaturity'

Despite her traumatic experiences with Sean, Madonna had become a much calmer and more confident person in herself,

according to Pat Leonard. "I've seen her change a lot in the last two years. When it first all turned up, she kept fighting to make sure it didn't go away. Now there's a lot more trusting. She doesn't think it's gonna go away."

"I have more bills, my telephone rings more, I look down at the ground more when I'm walking and I take people out to dinner more," said Madonna of her success in 1986, "and sometimes I get this scary feeling that I could do anything I wanted ..."

Madonna now had three multi-million selling albums to her credit and, after a crash course in driving, had bought a blue Mercedes sports coupé in which to cruise around LA. Her Malibu home was her sanctuary, "When I go up my driveway, that's where I draw the line. Wherever I live, that should be sacred. I get frightened sometimes when fans are relentless and they never leave us alone ... people hang out at the bottom of our driveway and constantly ring our doorbell."

And after 10 years of going it alone, Madonna was really close to her family again. In the December issue of *Life* magazine, she posed with her seven attractive brothers and sisters: Martin, Anthony, Christopher, Mario, Paula, Melanie and Jennifer, all hugging and squeezing each other. "Now I'm an established artist, I think my father really understands what I was trying to do," says Madonna. "Nowadays he's very happy and proud of me."

But the fans weren't the only ones drowning their sorrows. Madonna had hyped herself up for a performance and had never had to cancel a show before. As she tried to wind down and boost team morale by dining at a Japanese Italian restaurant, she experienced one of the most extraordinary and moving encounters she had ever had with a fan. Somehow a little Japanese girl had managed to track Madonna down to the restaurant and burst inside hugging a batch of souvenir programmes. Soaked to the skin, shaking with emotion and struggling to get her words out she pleaded, 'Please, please, so sorry, so sorry . . .'' The room went silent with anticipation.

Madonna beckoned her over and as she started to sign the programmes, the girl starting bowing and bursting into tears, setting off some of the band and crew. It was a poignant scene that both touched and disturbed Madonna. "When people make themselves that vulnerable, they always endear themselves to me. And yet there was something so servile about it, sometimes it makes you feel like you're enslaving somebody. And that's a creepy feeling."

That night, hundreds of fans found their way to the hotel where Madonna was staying, and sat up chanting her name. Madonna meant so much to them. "I think I stand for everything that they're taught not to be, so maybe I provide them with a little bit of encouragement." When the rain stopped and the Who's That Girl Tour finally got underway, Madonna stepped out from behind a screen in her revealing black bodice and fishnet tights thinking: "You have a big responsibility, because they're all out there to get something from you . . ."

She gave them the encouragement they craved with a spectacular stage-set, elaborate costume changes, sexy show-woman-ship and, as ever, that wonderful sense of humour. There were serious messages too. For 'Papa Don't Preach', pictures of pious churches and His Holiness The Pope were projected onto screens, and for 'Where's The Party', a newspaper dropped down at the back of the set with the giant headline, MADONNA: I'M NOT ASHAMED. It spoke volumes. And then there was the ballad 'Live To Tell' for which a giant photo of Madonna was projected

above her, and as the photo faded, she fell to the floor in a gesture of hopelessness – then sprang back up again in defiance – the girl in the gutter, always fighting back and aiming for the stars.

Rolling Stone magazine went to Japan with Madonna and praised her fine performance. "There has probably never been a more imaginative or forceful showcase for the feminine sensibility in pop than Madonna's current concert tour," wrote their reviewer. "She is simply the first female entertainer who has ever starred in a show of this scope, a fusion of Broadway-style choreography and post-disco song and dance that tops the standards set by previous live concert firebrands like Prince and Michael Jackson."

Ironically, as Madonna told *Rolling Stone* that she was sure that Sean was finally beginning to realise that violence was a waste of energy, the very day she returned to Los Angeles she read in a newspaper that he had been sentenced to 60 days in jail for punching an extra during the filming of his new movie, *Colors*. He had also been arrested for reckless driving which complicated matters even further. "At the time I didn't know all the details, and I didn't want to."

Sean was awarded a few weeks' reprieve to finish filming in West Germany but violated the agreement by flying to New York to see the special Aids Benefit concert Madonna gave at Madison Square Garden as a tribute to the memory of her dear friend Martin Burgoyne, who had recently died of the terrible disease. So much support had come from the gay, black and Latin communities, the groups hit hardest by Aids in the early days, that Madonna wanted to try and do something for them.

"I'm trying to think of something eloquent to say," she told her audience, "but I don't want this to be a morbid event. Hopefully your presence and our help together will help us find a cure for this thing forever."

The benefit raised over a quarter of a million dollars but the press responded with their unswerving, jaundiced judgements. *The New York Times* missed the point completely and slammed her show, calling it "shallow, kitschy pop entertainment." Madonna shrugged off the criticism commenting: "There are still those people who, no matter what I do, will always think of me as a little disco tart."

And then there were the rumours that Sean was furious with Madonna for picking up Burgoyne's hospital bills and that he had demanded she take an Aids test. There were rumours that they had had a big bust-up before the concert which had affected her performance. There were rumours that Sean's possessions were being moved in and out of the Penn household as frequently as he threw punches, and that they were getting divorced – again.

One thing was for sure, a warrant had been issued for Sean's arrest in LA unless he returned to Europe promptly to keep his part of the bargain and finish his filming. And there was no escaping the jail sentence, though the press had everyone believe that Sean was marched into a luxury jail and given the star treatment throughout his short stay.

"All the talk was heightened dramatics," said Madonna. "We are a Hollywood couple, so people are going to pay a lot of attention to our marriage. If we have fights, I think that's pretty normal for young people in their first few years of marriage, especially when you have to put up with all the pressures we've been under. I think the fact that we're still together is pretty amazing. You

know, we're working it out. It's easy to give up, but it's not easy for me to give up."

In August 18, just two days after her 28th birthday, Madonna forgave England for its hostile treatment towards her when she filmed the doomed *Shanghai Surprise*, and returned to play for her UK fans. The press built up her tour for days before her arrival with Madonna fashion spreads and imaginative Madonna diet sheets. All 144,000 tickets for her first two shows sold out in 18 hours and the extra dates needed no advertising. She played to 296,000 people in Britain opening at Roundhay Park, Leeds in Yorkshire for one night, followed by three nights at Wembley Stadium, where touts were selling £15 tickets for £30 outside.

Madonna jogged daily with a bodyguard during her stay, and the flabby paparazzi tried in vain to keep pace. *Penthouse* magazine flexed its sordid muscles again by digging up more nudes for the delight of Madonna's gawping male fans. When a gang of uncouth English louts started chanting "Get your tits out for the lads" at the Leeds concert, Madonna handled the situation brilliantly by feigning embarrassment. "Oh my god, you're singing a dirty song! Stop it or you'll make me blush . . . you forget about my tits, they belong to me." And when it threatened to rain during a show she flirted, "Gee it's cold up here, but I want us to keep each other warm. Don't touch the person next to you though, or I'll get jealous."

With the end of the tour came a temporary halt to Madonna's recording career. She announced she would be taking a long break to concentrate on films, and she had even set up her own production company, Siren Films, as a creative investment. The big question on everyone's lips was, had she given up music for good?

"After the Who's That Girl Tour I said to myself, 'Hey, I don't ever want to hear any of my songs ever again and I don't know whether I'll ever write another one.' I returned feeling so burned out and I was convinced I wouldn't go near music for quite a while. But Pat Leonard built this new studio and I went to see it – within an hour we'd written this great song. It amazed me." Leonard had managed to entice Madonna back into the music business.

"Sure, there have been times when I've thought 'If I'd known it was going to be like this, I wouldn't have tried so hard.' Being a star is both scary and exciting, because who knows what will come of it, what things I'll gain and what things will be taken away? I mean, you just don't know until you get there ..."

In 1988, Madonna-bashing went out of fashion – but only because the girl had kept a very low profile of late. This was her chance to have a rest, or a holiday, but no ... "I'd like to have the ability to sit still and do nothing without getting totally neurotic. I occasionally force myself to do that, cold turkey, but it's incredibly hard for me." Instead Madonna challenged herself to fly alone to New York. "It was the first time I'd done anything like that in a long time because I usually travel with my secretary or some kind of security person. I was so frightened. People are crazy and they think they know you and they won't leave you alone. But I ended up sitting next to a very nice guy in advertising. He knew who I was because people kept coming up for autographs.

"It's healthy for me to force myself to move about independently. It helps me touch base with reality ... I could never live a sheltered life. That would drive me insane."

In April, along with 30 other actresses, Madonna auditioned for a new play by David Mamet called *Speed-The-Plow*. Mamet sent everyone home, save Madonna, announcing she had read the part 'beautifully'. It wasn't her first flirtation with play-acting: she had appeared in a rather secret project at New York's Lincoln Center workshop called *Goose And Tomtom* in which she played a gangster's moll. As the press had been banned, the play received little attention, though word leaked that Madonna was 'mesmerising'.

Mamet's play was a tough comedy about American, and in particular, Hollywood values. Madonna's part was the role of a 'temporary girl', who doesn't really have a clue what she's doing, but stands in anyway when the secretary of a Hollywood head of production is indisposed. The production head has a bet with a friend that he can seduce his temp, and though Madonna knows exactly what he's up to, she shows up at his home –

Arriving for an early *Speed The Plow*
rehearsal in New York,
script in hand.

Curtain call for the first night
preview of Speed The Plow; left to right –
Joe Mantegna, Madonna and Roy Silver.

and a modern Beauty And The Beast fable ensues as the naïve 'temporary girl' proceeds to outsmart the worldly businessman.

On May 4, *Speed-The-Plow* opened on Broadway and this time the press, greedy for a new Madonna slanging match, were actually allowed in. Why not? Madonna knew just what their reactions would be, and was determined not to give a damn. "I've become much more tolerant of people and human error. Being constantly scrutinized and criticised as I am, you simply have to become tolerant – and a bit passive."

Madonna's fans waited anxiously outside the Royale Theatre stage door to catch a glimpse of their idol, whom they still kept voting to the top of the yearly pop polls, despite her not having made a record in ages.

Security inside the theatre was unusually heavy for a Broadway production and when a member of the audience tried to nip off in the middle of the first act, he had to explain himself to an over-zealous bouncer.

When Madonna made her entrance in a modest suit, with her newly dyed reddish brown hair, no one seemed to recognise her at first. When she took her final bow she refused to recognise the so-called importance of the newspaper reviews, that the rest of the cast were waiting anxiously to read at the celebration party. She didn't miss much: "Her ineptitude is scandalously thorough," commented a CBS TV reviewer, "The woman cannot move on stage. She cannot give meaning to the words she is saying. I've never before seen on a Broadway stage someone who didn't have the basic elements of acting." "NO, SHE CAN'T ACT", screamed the *New York Daily News* headline with a review that ran: "Elegantly designed, impeccably directed, *Speed-The-Plow* is Mamet's clearest, wittiest play. I bet it would be even funnier with an actress." Only the *New York Times* gracefully declined to admit that her début represented "intelligent, scrupulously disciplined comic acting." And the reputable British *Guardian* newspaper gave a positively glowing review, comparing Madonna to her old friend Monroe: "She plays what looks like Mamet's version of the early Marilyn, who also had an ambition to star on Broadway . . ."

But perhaps the unkindest cut of all was a theory voiced in theatrical circles as to why Madonna got the part in the first place. It was suggested that writer David Mamet approved the choice of Madonna in his play about the moral emptiness of the American entertainment industry precisely because Madonna perfectly epitomised such a void.

In actuality Madonna wrote Mamet a fan letter after watching his film direction début *House Of Games*, expressing a wish to work with him at some time. When she heard that the *Speed-The-Plow* rôle was up for grabs, she asked for an audition which director Gregory Mosher described as 'decisive'. "It's scary how much talent she has. You cannot take your eyes off her when she is on stage," he told the *Daily News*.

Madonna had made another dream come true. So many people feel that the spirit of Monroe lives on in Madonna's quest for recognition – but how does she truly feel about the reality of becoming an eighties icon?

"It isn't all the way I dreamed it when I was a little girl. How could I dream all this? It's just bigger than anything I could ever imagine. It's hard work. I guess you have to have a very large ego and a good tolerance for pain. You have to be addicted to work and

keep going and going and going – even when you're tired or sick and you can't go on stage – but you have to. When you work really hard on something and it doesn't come out the way you wanted it to, and you've put your blood and guts into it for months and months – that's pain. But you learn from it, so it's worth it."

Madonna the little girl from Michigan; Madonna the teenage New Yorker; Madonna the dancer; Madonna the pop star; Madonna the actress; Madonna the star who just opened on Broadway; . . . who is the real Madonna? And does she ever step back and ask that same question herself?

On the Who's That Girl Tour, the focal part of her act used to be that part of the show where Madonna sang 'Live To Tell', and then halted in the middle of the song to gaze thoughtfully up at the huge picture of herself which glowed above her head. What was she thinking then?

"I used to look at it and say, 'Oh God, what have I done? What have I created? Is 'that' me or is 'this' me, this small person standing down here on the stage? That's why I called the tour Who's That Girl: because I play a lot of characters and every time I do a video or a film, people go, 'Oh, that's what she's like.' And I'm not any of them. I'm all of them. I'm none of them. You know what I mean . . . ?"

"I have twinges of regret, but I feel more sadness than anything. Feeling regret is really destructive. I have learned a great deal from my marriage, so much. About everything – mostly about myself."

n January 5th 1989 – despite the brave front she had put on her marriage for its short but tempestuous three and a half year span; deflecting all the tabloid rumours of a break-up (which started just one week after the wedding) and holding tightly onto her hopes for a way to work things out – Madonna finally stopped fighting and filed for divorce.

Had she failed the test of love, or had it failed her? When you consider Madonna's normally unbreakable spirit, and the Catholic guilt-trip she would inevitably suffer for such a sin – the going with Sean Penn must have been tough indeed. Whereas Madonna

has a reputation for channelling any anger or pain she feels into her work, and learning and growing from it, Penn's reputation was simply to lash out – so had the punches started rolling again?

Madonna cited 'irreconcilable differences' for the split. The press cited violence in an alleged 'NIGHT OF TERROR' that took place in their Malibu home. Madonna charged the press with making it all up. The press charged Sean with assault, and painted a graphic picture of an ugly domestic scene in which Sean was supposed to have tied Madonna to a chair for nine hours, attacked her, and even threatened to stick her head in the oven. Madonna managed to escape to the sheriff's office and the police surrounded the house. Sean accused Madonna of making it all up. The truth is that charges were actually filed by her on that night of December 28th – and dropped a few days later – and there is no smoke without fire.

Madonna once said, of life in general, "I'd rather walk through a fire than away from one." Now, in the aftermath of her divorce she told *Rolling Stone* magazine "Well, Sean's fire, that's for sure . . . we were two fires rubbing up against each other. It's exciting and difficult."

The friction that their marriage had thrived on, had eventually burnt it out. Madonna refused to discuss the sordid details of the final melt-down – she was later to express them musically. "People want to hear the dirt but this is not really anything I want to talk about . . . . It's totally unfair to Sean. I have great respect for him. It's like most relationships that fail. It's not one thing. It's many things that go on over a period of time. It's been a slow breaking point all the way."

Madonna's old friend Steve Bray, who had got along well with Penn, confirmed her feelings. "I think it was just two people who were basically incompatible at the end. They tried very, very hard to make their relationship work but in the end there was something inherently incompatible in their natures."

Madonna's father Sylvio was there for her in her hour of need; gone are the days when Madonna felt she had to prove she could get by without him, because she was so hurt when he married again after her mother's death. "We've made our way back into each other's lives . . . I have a million different feelings about my father, but mostly I love him to death." Madonna's mother was there for her too, in an ethereal kind of way. "I talk to her often . . . I don't know if she can hear me or not, but I tell her things that a girl can only say to her mother. Private things."

Throughout the ordeal, Madonna continued to appear as a temporary girl in *Speed The Plow*, a role she no longer relished, for that too had become something of a love/hate relationship. Because of her pulling power, a ticket for Mamet's play was one of the hardest to get on Broadway but when, after nine months, the curtain fell for the final time in February, she revealed, "It was just gruelling having to do the same thing every night, playing a character who is so unlike me . . . it just got to me after a while. I was becoming as miserable as the character I played."

Madonna said goodbye to Broadway and headed for her new home, a hilltop sanctuary in the Hollywood Hills. It was

time to whip up some of that old Madonna mania again. Two new projects lay immediately ahead, a new album and a new film.

Teaming up with Steve Bray and Pat Leonard, Madonna set about some musical healing by exorcising her emotional and religious wounds with an album that was to be analysed with intrigue by the music critics, keen to unlock the secrets of its autobiographical content. All agreed it was a work of maturity and depth and, yes, perhaps even a work of art from the former lightweight disco siren.

Dedicated to her mother, "who taught me how to pray", the melodies and lyrics flowed like milk and honey from the writing team, who found they had an album's worth of songs in a matter of weeks. "We wrote 'Like A Prayer', 'Spanish Eyes', 'Till Death Do Us Part', 'Dear Jessie', 'Promise To Try' and 'Cherish' in a two-week period," boasts Pat Leonard.

"He throws the music at me and I listen to it over and over again," explains Madonna, "and somehow the music suggests words to me . . . other times I will come to Pat with an idea for a song, either lyrically or emotionally, or I'll have a melody line in my head."

Steve Bray worked the same way with Madonna on the tracks 'Express Yourself' and 'Keep It Together', and two love songs called 'First Is A Kiss' and 'Love Attack' that were finally rejected because they didn't suit the somewhat confessional mood of the album.

"This was an album she needed to do, I'm sure of it," comments Bray. "It was a cathartic kind of thing to do. If she's in love she'll write love songs. If she's not in love she definitely won't be writing love songs. That's why the love songs we recorded aren't on the LP – she didn't feel that they were real enough for her at the time."

What was real was a lot of pain and anguish, with Sean, with childhood family memories and religion. It was time to start nailing a few Catholic colours to the mast and throwing darts at them again, and this Madonna did with a spectacularly scandalous video for the single release of 'Like A Prayer'. It was to cause a rumpus on the scale of 'Like A Virgin' and 'Papa Don't Preach' for its 'immoral' content.

The build-up during April for the new single was exciting. The wholesome Pepsi Cola company announced that they had adopted Madonna as their new icon for their fizzy drink, previously championed by Michael Jackson. She would reportedly earn five million dollars for a one-year contract, to include commercials and tour sponsorship for a world tour. 'Like A Prayer' was used in a Pepsi advert in which Madonna was featured watching an old home movie of herself as a child blowing out the candles on a birthday cake, with

Madonna the woman encouraging Madonna the little girl to "Go on . . . make a wish." The enchanting advert was a success, Pepsi loved it and Madonna was proud of it.

"I considered it a challenge to make a commercial that had some sort of artistic value. I like the challenge of merging art and commerce. As far as I'm concerned, making a video is also a commercial. The Pepsi spot is a great and different way to expose the record."

But everything backfired. Madonna's own video for 'Like A Prayer' saw her gyrating in front of a scene of blazing crucifixes, dancing herself into a trance-like frenzy with a gospel choir, and kissing the feet of a black image of Christ that magically came to life in the church.

The actual storyline was very moral; white girl witnesses street crime and sees black youth falsely accused. She runs into a nearby church (but not before the real villain has caught sight of her face) where she wrestles with her conscience. Should she go to the police and present herself as a witness, even though this could endanger her own life?

After much soul searching, she decides to do her moral duty, and the black youth is released. But the video was certified 'blasphemous', music shows cut the offending scenes before airing it, and the Pepsi deal went flat.

It seemed like another case of female victimisation in the music business, for it had been okay for Michael Jackson to make a video that went against the grain of his religion – the famous 'Thriller' with its dancing, flesh-eating, zombies rising from the grave to torment the living. If Pepsi could stomach Jackson's gory, horror frenzy, then why all the fuss about Madonna's religious fantasy?

Nevertheless, the question had to be asked – had Madonna, with commerce-aforethought, pulled the old religious rabbit out of the hat again because she had been away for over a year, and usurped by the likes of young Debbie Gibson and Kylie Minogue? Pat Leonard, who was himself raised by a Catholic family, didn't feel that Madonna had made the video to deliberately cause a fuss. However, he

didn't think she'd mind it! "She's always willing to deal with whatever reaction people have. Obviously if you're on a hill dancing with half a dozen burning crosses behind you, someone's going to say something!"

Madonna defended herself by pointing out that any shock value was in the minds of the beholders. "The video had a very positive message. It was about overcoming racism and overcoming the fear of telling the truth. So many people are afraid to stand out on a limb and stand up for someone else . . . it dealt with a lot of taboos and I think the people who reacted negatively to it were afraid of their own feelings that they have about those issues."

Perhaps the real issue in the video was Madonna's own inability to overcome the feelings of guilt that had been instilled in her as a Catholic – in terms of your feelings of guilt and remorse and whether you've sinned or not. Sometimes I'm racked with guilt when I needn't be . . . in Catholicism you are born a sinner and you are a sinner all of your life."

Madonna still prays, though insists the ritual has nothing to do with religion, acting instead as a kind of self-help therapy to balance out life's ups and downs. "I pray when I feel any sort of extreme. I pray when I feel so great that I'll think I need to check in with myself and recognise how good life is . . . when I'm feeling really bad or sad, I pray to reassure myself. It's all a kind of rationalisation."

T he album 'Like A Prayer' was released in a whirl of successful publicity, and with the pungent whiff of patchouli oil scenting every cover, at considerable expense to Madonna, and for reasons known only to her. Still, 1989 had proved to be the long awaited 'second summer of love' and the mood was peace and love. Her LP cover optimistically reflected those sentiments as the famous Madonna stomach exposed itself again, framed by hippie baubles and beads. The lyrical content, so easily grasped by the fans who knew Madonna's life story, was painstakingly dissected by the music press, for this was an album in which Madonna had also chosen to expose her soul.

"The overall emotional context of the album is drawn from what I was going through when I was growing up – and I'm still growing up. It definitely does have a very strong feminine point of view . . . I've had some painful experiences with men in my life . . ."

'He takes a drink, she goes inside/ He starts to scream, the vases fly' run the lyrics for 'Till Death Do Us Part', a song that seemed to echo certain elements of that so-called NIGHT OF TERROR. An accusative finger points directly to Sean Penn. "Like most of the songs on my album, it's very much drawn from my life, factually speaking, but it's fictionalised too. 'Till Death Do Us Part' is about a destructive relationship that is powerful and painful. In this song, however, it's a cycle that you can't get out of until you die . . . now that's where the truth stops, because I would never want to continue a terrible relationship forever and ever and ever until I die."

Another song on the album about a love-hate relationship is 'Love Song', a duet she did with Prince, whom she met on tour in San Francisco back in 1985. "We've been friends for years and admirerers of each other's work so we'd always talked about getting together to write." Prince and Madonna had considered writing a whole musical together when she went to his studio in Minnesota to work on material, " . . . but we didn't really finish anything." However, when Prince turned up in New York to see *Speed The Plow*, he brought Madonna a rough mix of one of the songs they'd worked on. "I thought it was just fabulous."

Determined to put it on the album, tapes were sent back and forth between Los Angeles and Minnesota and played over the phone. "I loved working that way. I played the keyboards myself and because I don't know

mermaids from the land of make believe, and it's almost a psychedelic tribute to that first record she ever bought, 'Incense and Peppermints' by Strawberry Alarm Clock. The song was actually named after Pat Leonard's then three-and-a-half-year-old daughter. "Madonna and Jessie have been friends since she was born," says Leonard. "Madonna's a godmother almost . . . Jessie listens to the album and announces proudly 'it's my song'."

'Express Yourself', 'Keep It Together' and 'Cherish' provide the light relief on the album as pop songs, pure and simple; the first two are Madonna's tributes to a past musical influence, Sly and The Family Stone. 'Express Yourself' was chosen as the second, summer single release.

that much, it kind of came out strange and interesting . . . " it was another ode to Sean. "It's really about that push and pull of a relationship. The back and forth. I love you, I hate you. I want you, get away from me. You build me up and tear me down. That constant rubbing."

The anti-male theme continued. Next in the firing line stood the authoritarian father figures of the world, be they natural or spiritual. 'You can't hurt me now/I got away from you, I never thought I would', sings Madonna in 'Oh Father'. Musically, this was Madonna's " . . . tribute to Simon and Garfunkel, whom I loved."

God's existence is questioned in 'Spanish Eyes', and yet one more song, a strange concoction at the end of the album, takes a cheeky stab at Catholicism. 'Act Of Contrition', described on the sleeve notes as being 'produced by the powers that be', features Prince's guitar work, and was born out of spontaneity. Pat Leonard remembers its

conception: "The engineer flipped over the tape of 'Like A Prayer' and played it backwards and Madonna just sat there with the microphone and said a prayer . . . I don't think 'Act Of Contrition' is intended to offend anyone, just to be fun."

Madonna returns to the bitter-sweet days of Little Nonni's childhood with the song 'Promise To Try" in which she confronts the death of her mother with the lyrics 'Don't let memory play games with your mind/She's a faded smile in frozen time,' compensating for such a tragic loss, Madonna had, quite naturally, distorted and fantasised her mother's memory over the years – perhaps building her into something she never was. "It's about letting go of that . . . it's about a yearning to have her in my life but also about trying to accept the fact that she's not."

In contrast, 'Dear Jessie' is about the wonders of childhood, the 'Pink elephants and lemonade', the fairies, leprechauns, and

The video was set in a steamy, sweaty factory. The atmosphere was pure Metropolis, as in the famous 1926 futuristic film. And Madonna was a blonde again – against her will – but her forthcoming role in Warren Beatty's film, *Dick Tracy*, had demanded fair hair.

Madonna had begged Beatty not to make her do it. "I felt kind of great having my own hair colour for the first time in years. And then I had to change it so I had a bit of an identity crisis. Being blonde is definitely a different state of mind . . . I feel more grounded, and Italian when I have dark hair, and I feel more ethereal when I have light hair . . . being blonde has some incredible sort of sexual connotation. Men really respond to it."

Madonna took her rediscovered sirendom to the limit by exposing virtually every inch of herself in the video for 'Express Yourself'. Not since the *Playboy/Penthouse* war had so many seen so much of her. Gyrating in black stockings, suspenders and a corset, thrusting and grabbing at her crotch, crawling across the floor to lick milk from a saucer, lying chained to a bed, and sitting naked on satin sheets – Madonna made no bones about the sexual connotations. And yet, the overall effect was remarkably subtle and enjoyable, and it was a video she had masterminded.

"I oversaw everything – the building of the sets, everyone's costume, I had meetings with make-up and hair and the cinematographer, casting . . . kind of like making a little movie . . . the ultimate thing behind the song is that if you don't express yourself, if you don't say what you want, then you're not going to get it. And in effect you are chained down by your inability to say what you feel or go after what you want."

One thing Madonna still wanted, desperately, was to be taken seriously as an actress. In Warren Beatty's film, *Dick Tracy*, she hoped she had finally found the vehicle that would make this possible. "I've learned that if you surround yourself with great writers and great actors and a great director . . . it's pretty hard to go wrong. In the past I've been in a really big hurry to make movies and I haven't taken the time to make sure all of those elements were in line. It's a waste of time doing something mediocre."

It was to be her first film role as a villain. "Breathless Mahoney is a siren and a nightclub singer," says Madonna describing her character, "and she falls in love with Dick Tracy in spite of herself. I don't think she's inherently evil, but she's quite accomplished in her villainy."

In 1989 the word on everyone's lips was that Madonna had become romantically involved with Warren Beatty. A close friendship had certainly formed, for they had been seen and snapped together on numerous occasions. Madonna did not care to comment on her new companion. The sad truth was that she blamed herself, in part, for the demise of her marriage, because she had been so eager to tell the whole world about her love and intimate feelings for Sean – setting their relationship up for a fall.

"I wanted the whole world to know that this was the man I loved more than anything . . . but the romantic side of me wanting to announce my love, given my position in life, would ultimately work against me in the future . . . once you reveal it to the world, you give it up, and it's not your own anymore. You let people know about the great things and they want the dirt too, so you never get left alone. I now realise how important it is to hold on to privacy and keeping things to yourself."

1989 was a year of new beginnings for Madonna, a year of starting over where relationships, music and movies were concerned. She had reclaimed her rightful place at the top of the charts with her long-awaited album, and the singles 'Like A Prayer', 'Express Yourself', 'Cherish', and the Christmas release of 'Dear Jessie'. But more than that, she had proved herself to be the ultimate idol of the decade – and the ultimate woman of the eighties.

COMPLETE MADONNA UK DISCOGRAPHY

SINGLES

Warner Bros. W 9899	**EVERYBODY**/dub version (December 1982)	
Warner Bros. W 9899T	**EVERYBODY**/dub version (12", December 1982)	
Sire W 9522	**LUCKY STAR/I KNOW IT** (September 1983, PS)	
Sire W 9522T	**LUCKY STAR/I KNOW IT** (12", September 1983, PS)	
Sire W 9405	**HOLIDAY/THINK OF ME** (November 1983, PS; No. 6)	
Sire W 9405T	**HOLIDAY/THINK OF ME** (12", November 1983, PS)	
Sire W 9522	**LUCKY STAR/I KNOW IT** (March 1984, PS, No. 14)	
Sire W 9522T	**LUCKY STAR/I KNOW IT** (12", March 1984, PS)	
Sire W 9260	**BORDERLINE/PHYSICAL ATTRACTION** (June 1984, PS, No. 56)	
Sire W 9260T	**BORDERLINE/PHYSICAL ATTRACTION** (12", June 1984, PS)	
Sire W 9210	**LIKE A VIRGIN/STAY** (September 1984, PS, No. 3)	
Sire W 9210T	**LIKE A VIRGIN/STAY** (12", September 1984, PS)	
Sire W 9083	**MATERIAL GIRL/PRETENDER** (February 1985, poster sleeve, No. 3)	
Sire W 9083	**MATERIAL GIRL/PRETENDER** (February 1985, PS)	
Sire W 9083T	**MATERIAL GIRL/PRETENDER** (12", February 1985)	
Geffen A 6323	**CRAZY FOR YOU**/I'll Fall in Love Again by Sammy Hagar (June 1985, No. 2, PS)	
Geffen A 6323P	**CRAZY FOR YOU**/I'll Fall In Love Again (June 1985, shaped picture disc)	
Sire W 8934	**INTO THE GROOVE/SHOO-BEE-DOO** (July 1985, PS, No. 1)	
Sire W 8934T	**INTO THE GROOVE/SHOO-BEE-DOO/EVERYBODY** (12", July 1985, PS)	
Sire W 8934P	**INTO THE GROOVE/SHOO-BEE-DOO** (July 1985, shaped picture disc)	
Sire W 9405	**HOLIDAY/THINK OF ME** (July 1985, PS, No. 2)	
Sire W 9405T	**HOLIDAY/THINK OF ME** (12", July 1985, PS)	
Sire W 9405P	**HOLIDAY/THINK OF ME** (July 1985, picture disc 12")	
Sire W 8881	**ANGEL/BURNING UP** (September 1985, PS, No. 5)	
Sire W 8881T	**ANGEL/BURNING UP/ANGEL** (DANCE MIX) (12", September 1985, PS)	
Sire W 8881P	**ANGEL/BURNING UP** (September 1985, shaped picture disc 12")	
Geffen A 6585	**THE GAMBLER**/Nature Of The Beast by Black 'n' Blue (October 1985, poster sleeve, No. 4)	
Geffen A 6585	**THE GAMBLER**/Nature Of The Beast (October 1985, PS)	
Geffen TA 6585	**THE GAMBLER**/Nature Of The Beast/**THE GAMBLER** (EXTENDED DANCE MIX)/**THE GAMBLER** (INSTRUMENTAL) (12", October 1985, PS)	
Sire W 8848	**DRESS YOU UP/I KNOW IT** (November 1985, PS, No. 5)	
Sire W 8848T	**DRESS YOU UP/I KNOW IT/DRESS YOU UP** (CASUAL INSTRUMENTAL MIX) (12", November 1985, PS)	
Sire W 8848T	**DRESS YOU UP/I KNOW IT/DRESS YOU UP** (12" poster sleeve, 11/85)	
Sire W 8848P	**DRESS YOU UP/I KNOW IT/DRESS YOU UP** (12" shaped pic disc, 11/85)	
Sire W 9260	**BORDERLINE/PHYSICAL ATTRACTION** (January 1986, PS, No. 2)	
Sire W 9260P	**BORDERLINE/PHYSICAL ATTRACTION** (January 1986, shaped pic disc)	
Sire W 9260T	**BORDERLINE/PHYSICAL ATTRACTION/BORDERLINE** (DUB) (12" January 1986, PS)	
Sire W 8717	**LIVE TO TELL/LIVE TO TELL** (INSTRUMENTAL) (April 1986, PS, No. 2)	
Sire W 8717T	**LIVE TO TELL** (EXTENDED)/**LIVE TO TELL** (INSTRUMENTAL)/**LIVE TO TELL** (EDITED VERSION) (12", April 1986, PS)	
Sire W 8636	**PAPA DON'T PREACH/AIN'T NO BIG DEAL** (June 1986, PS, No. 1)	
Sire W 8636T	**PAPA DON'T PREACH/AIN'T NO BIG DEAL** (12", June 1986, PS)	
Sire W 8636P	**PAPA DON'T PREACH/AIN'T NO BIG DEAL** (12" pic disc, June 1986)	
Sire W 8550	**TRUE BLUE/HOLIDAY** (September 1986, PS, No. 1)	
Sire W 8550T	**TRUE BLUE** (LONG VERSION)/**HOLIDAY** (LP VERSION) (12", September '86, PS)	
Sire W 8550P	**TRUE BLUE/HOLIDAY** (12" picture disc, September 1986)	
Sire W 8480	**OPEN YOUR HEART** (REMIX)/**LUCKY STAR** (December 1986, PS, No. 4)	
Sire W 8480T	**OPEN YOUR HEART** (EXTENDED)/**LUCKY STAR** (EXTENDED)/**OPEN YOUR HEART** (DUB MIX) (12", December 1986)	
Sire W 8378	**LA ISLA BONITA/LA ISLA BONITA** (INSTRUMENTAL) (March 1987, No. 1)	
Sire W 8378T	**LA ISLA BONITA/LA ISLA BONITA** (INSTRUMENTAL) (12", March 1987)	
Sire W 8341	**WHO'S THAT GIRL/WHITE HEAT** (July 1987, No. 1)	
Sire W 8341T	**WHO'S THAT GIRL/WHITE HEAT** (12", July 1987)	
Sire W 8224	**CAUSING A COMMOTION/JIMMY JIMMY** (September 1987, No. 4)	
Sire W 8224T	**CAUSING A COMMOTION/JIMMY JIMMY** (12", September 1987)	
Sire W 8224P	**CAUSING A COMMOTION/JIMMY JIMMY** (12" picture disc, September 1987)	
Sire W 8115	**THE LOOK OF LOVE/I KNOW IT** (October 1987, No. 9)	
Sire W 8115T	**THE LOOK OF LOVE/I KNOW IT** (12", October 1987)	
Sire W 8115P	**THE LOOK OF LOVE/I KNOW IT** (12" picture disc, October 1987)	
Baktabak BAKPAK 1012	**INTERVIEW PICTURE DISC** (set of four 7" singles in wallet, December 1988)	
WEA W7539	**LIKE A PRAYER/ACT OF CONTRITION** (March 1989)	
WEA W7539T	**LIKE A PRAYER** (EXTENDED)/**LIKE A PRAYER** (CLUB MIX)/**ACT OF CONTRITION** (12", March 1989)	
WEA W7539CD	**LIKE A PRAYER/LIKE A PRAYER** (CLUB MIX)/**LIKE A PRAYER** (EXTENDED) (CD, March 1989)	
WEA W7539C	**LIKE A PRAYER/LIKE A PRAYER** (CLUB MIX)/**LIKE A PRAYER** (EXTENDED) (cassette, March 1989)	
WEA W7539TP	**LIKE A PRAYER/LIKE A PRAYER** (CLUB MIX)/**LIKE A PRAYER** (EXTENDED) (12" picture disc, March 1989)	
WEA 7539TX	**LIKE A PRAYER/LIKE A PRAYER** (12" DANCE MIX)/**LIKE A PRAYER** (CHURCHAPELLA MIX) (12", March 1989)	
Replay 3000	**COSMIC CLIMB**/(INSTRUMENTAL) (12", April 1989)	
WEA W2948	**EXPRESS YOURSELF/THE LOOK OF LOVE** (May, 1989)	

WEA W2948T	**EXPRESS YOURSELF/EXPRESS YOURSELF** (NON-STOP EXPRESS MIX)/**EXPRESS YOURSELF** (STOP AND GO MIX) (12", May 1989)	
WEA W2948C	**EXPRESS YOURSELF/THE LOOK OF LOVE** (cassette, May 1989)	
WEA W2948TD	**EXPRESS YOURSELF/EXPRESS YOURSELF** (NON-STOP EXPRESS MIX)/**EXPRESS YOURSELF** (STOP AND GO MIX) (12" picture disc, May 1989)	
WEA W2948CD	**EXPRESS YOURSELF/EXPRESS YOURSELF** (NON-STOP EXPRESS MIX)/**EXPRESS YOURSELF** (STOP AND GO MIX) (CD, May 1989)	
WEA 2948CX	**EXPRESS YOURSELF** (NON-STOP EXPRESS MIX)/**EXPRESS YOURSELF** (STOP AND GO MIX) (cassette, May 1989)	
Replay 3007	**TIME TO DANCE**/(INSTRUMENTAL) (12", June 1989)	
WEA W2883	**CHERISH/SUPERNATURAL** (August, 1989)	
WEA W2883T	**CHERISH** (EXTENDED)/**CHERISH/SUPERNATURAL** (12", August 1989)	
WEA W2883CD	**CHERISH** (EXTENDED)/**CHERISH/SUPERNATURAL** (CD, August 1989)	
WEA W2883C	**CHERISH/SUPERNATURAL** (cassette, August 1989)	
WEA W2883TC	**CHERISH** (EXTENDED)/**CHERISH/SUPERNATURAL** (12" picture disc, August 1989)	
Replay 3008	**ON THE STREET**/(INSTRUMENTAL) (12", September 1989)	
WEA W2668	**DEAR JESSIE/TILL DEATH DO US PART** (November 1989)	
WEA W2668T	**DEAR JESSIE/TILL DEATH DO US PART/HOLIDAY** (12" MIX) (12", November 1989)	
WEA W2668CD	**DEAR JESSIE/TILL DEATH DO US PART/HOLIDAY** (12" MIX) (CD, November 1989)	
WEA W2668C	**DEAR JESSIE/TILL DEATH DO US PART** (cassette, November 1989)	
WEA W2668T	**DEAR JESSIE/TILL DEATH DO US PART/HOLIDAY** (12" MIX) (12" in poster bag, November 1989)	
WEA W2668P	**DEAR JESSIE/TILL DEATH DO US PART** (picture disc, November 1989)	

All of Madonna's Sire 12" black vinyl singles from W 9522T to W8881T were reissued during 1986, with the exception of the original two-track version of "Borderline", which was replaced by the later three-track version. All of these reissues are still on catalogue.

ALBUMS

Sire 9238671	**MADONNA** (September 1983)	
Sire 9251571	**LIKE A VIRGIN** (November 1984)	
Sire WX 20	**LIKE A VIRGIN** (September 1985, with extra track, "Into The Groove")	
Sire WX 22	**THE FIRST ALBUM** (September 1985, repackaging of "Madonna")	
Sire WX 20P	**LIKE A VIRGIN** (September 1985, picture disc)	
Sire WX 54	**TRUE BLUE** (July 1986)	
Sire WX 54	**TRUE BLUE** (July 1986, blue vinyl with poster)	
Sire WX102	**WHO'S THAT GIRL** Film soundtrack (July 1987)	
Music & Media MAD 1001	**INTERVIEW PICTURE DISC** (February 1988)	
Baktabak BAK 2104	**INTERVIEW PICTURE DISC** (August 1988)	
WEA WX239	**LIKE A PRAYER** (March 1989)	
Receiver RRLP118	**THE EARLY YEARS** (October 1989)	

COMPACT DISCS

Sire 9251572	**LIKE A VIRGIN** (November 1984)	
Sire 9238672	**MADONNA** (November 1984)	
Sire 9251812	**LIKE A VIRGIN** (September 1985, with extra track, "Into The Groove")	
Sire 9254422	**TRUE BLUE** (July 1986)	
Sire 9256112	**WHO'S THAT GIRL** Film soundtrack (July 1987)	
WEA WX239CD	**LIKE A PRAYER** (March 1989)	
Receiver RRCD118	**THE EARLY YEARS** (October 1989)